North-South Technology Transfer
A Case Study of Petrochemicals in Latin America

A WORLD BANK RESEARCH PUBLICATION

North-South Technology Transfer

A Case Study of Petrochemicals in Latin America

Mariluz Cortes and Peter Bocock

Published for The World Bank
THE JOHNS HOPKINS UNIVERSITY PRESS
Baltimore and London

The Johns Hopkins University Press
Baltimore, Maryland 21218, U.S.A.

Editor: Jane Carroll
Binding design: Joyce Eisen

Library of Congress Cataloging in Publication Data

Cortes, Mariluz.
    North-South technology transfer.

    (A World Bank research publication)
    Bibliography: p.
    Includes index.
    1. Petroleum chemicals industry—Latin America.
2. Technology transfer—Latin America.   I. Bocock, Peter,
1942–   . II. World Bank.   III. Title.   IV. Series.
HD9579.C33L33   1984   338.4′7661804′098   83-49365
ISBN 0-8018-3259-4

Contents

Preface

The subject of this book—the transfer of industrial technology from developed to developing countries—has received increasing attention in recent years. As manufacturing production has become more widely diffused around the world and as the technological capacity of developing countries has come to be seen as one key to their overall economic development, economists and policymakers alike have begun to ask questions about the technology transfer process and its consequences. In particular, interest has focused on the extent to which transfer mechanisms affect the ability of recipients to acquire indigenous technological capability and to operate their plants independently of suppliers.

This book does not contribute directly to the debate about the consequences of technology transfers or their appropriateness—a debate that has sometimes seemed to generate more heat than light. Instead, after an initial review of some of the main conceptual issues involved, it focuses on a group of concrete prior questions: what are the main characteristics and concerns of technology suppliers and recipients, what kinds of contractual arrangements are in fact used for transfers, and what are the main factors that seem in practice to determine the use of one arrangement or another? Our aim is to illuminate the complexity of the mechanisms and motivations involved in the transfer process, a topic on which relatively little hard information is available.

As its title indicates, the book uses a case-study approach, concentrating on transfers in a particular technology-intensive industry—petrochemicals—and to a single relatively advanced region in the developing world—Latin America. The research on which it is based was undertaken by Cortes, first as a visiting research fellow at the Science Policy Research Unit (SPRU) at the University of Sussex, England, and subsequently as a staff member of the World Bank's Development Economics Department. Cortes's findings were condensed, reorganized, and compiled into their present form by Bocock, who also added some new material. The data underlying the analysis are derived from three sources:

- Technology agreements, engineering contracts, and investment and financing agreements for petrochemical plants in Latin America obtained directly from individuals in the countries concerned

- Information on the ownership of and sources of technology for 280 petrochemical plants in Latin America, obtained from trade journals (listed in the bibliography), from a Plant Index maintained by the SPRU, and from interviews with plant managers and officials in Latin American countries
- Further information obtained from interviews with personnel of the World Bank, the Inter-American Development Bank, and the United Nations Industrial Development Organization (UNIDO).

The information collected was cross-checked among these various sources to ensure its reliability, and was then used as the basis for the tables, the appendixes, and other factual data on petrochemicals in Latin America.

Many people have contributed to the preparation of this book for final publication. In particular, we would like to thank Professors Charles Cooper and Christopher Freeman of SPRU, who sponsored Cortes's original research; Ardy Stoutjesdijk, director of the World Bank's Development Economics Department, and Larry Westphal, chief of that department's Economics of Industry Division, both of whom encouraged us in the work that led to the book's completion in its present form; and Maria Ameal, Michiko Mitsuyasu, Kim Tran, and Ann Van Aken, all of whom helped to type the final draft.

Finally, several individuals have given us helpful comments at various stages in the book's preparation. In this connection we are again especially indebted to Larry Westphal, whose comprehensive and constructive review of the penultimate draft helped to clarify the text and saved us from a number of errors. Any remaining mistakes, whether of fact or interpretation, must be the responsibility of the authors alone.

MARILUZ CORTES
PETER BOCOCK

January 1984

North-South Technology Transfer

A Case Study of Petrochemicals in Latin America

Chapter 1

Introduction

This volume presents a descriptive study of the transfer of petrochemical technology to a group of industrializing countries in Latin America. It examines the principal characteristics of suppliers and recipients of petrochemical technology in the region and their prevailing attitudes with regard to transfers; illustrates some of the main features of the transfer process; and identifies the key factors which determine the particular transfer arrangements chosen under different circumstances. The study draws on empirical research covering 280 petrochemical plants in seven countries: Argentina, Brazil, Chile, Colombia, Mexico, Peru, and Venezuela. The twenty-six products manufactured in these plants made up most of Latin America's existing and planned output of high-volume petrochemicals (with the exception of some synthetic fibers) in 1976.

Purpose and Scope of the Study

Technology transfers between developed and developing countries have traditionally been viewed as potentially valuable shortcuts to more rapid economic advance in the latter. In recent years, however, both disillusioning practical experience and new analyses of the factors underlying the phenomenon of technological development have called into question the whole concept of the large-scale transfer of technology per se as a source of successful economic development. In addition, the terms and conditions under which a particular transfer takes place have come to be seen as critical determinants of its contribution to the long-term growth of the recipient entity and national economy. International organizations such as the Organisation for Economic Co-operation and Development (OECD), United Nations Conference on Trade and Development (UNCTAD), United Nations Industrial Development Organization (UNIDO), the U.N. Secretariat, and the World Bank have sponsored research on the subject, as have a number of academic institutions. Meanwhile, developing countries, both individually and as groups, have begun to take policy measures they believe necessary to bring transfer processes and mechanisms more into line with their development aims. Among the issues of special concern have been the appropriateness of some transfers of technology to the resource endowments, needs, and policy objectives of developing countries, and the possible adverse effects on recipients of some of the contractual arrangements under which transfers have taken place. Critics have suggested that particular arrangements have led to such consequences as:

- The manipulation of the income flows resulting from technology transfers to the private advantage of licensors
- An excessive degree of licensor influence over the units of production in recipient countries
- The inhibition of indigenous technological development in recipient countries and consequent continuation of their dependence on external sources of technology.

This book does not deal with the issue of appropriate technology, nor does it attempt systematically to prove or disprove the validity of concerns about the consequences of particular transfer arrangements. Instead it concentrates on the mechanics of the transfer process, trying to establish, in the context of the petrochemical industry, what is transferred, who participates in transfers and why, and under what terms and conditions transfers take place. The remainder of this chapter briefly sketches some of the concepts and classifications developed in the literature on technology transfer. Chapter 2 examines the nature and concerns of the main participants on the supply side of petrochemical technology transfers to Latin America. Chapter 3 discusses the structure of the petrochemical industry in Latin America, technology recipients' politics toward transfers, and local technological capabilities. Chapter 4 summarizes the principal issues raised in earlier sections and provides survey-based empirical data on the main factors determining the contractual arrangements used to acquire petrochemical technology for the 280 plants covered. Relevant statistical material is provided in text tables and in the appendixes.

The Conceptual Framework

One of the problems about discussing technology transfer is that the terms used in the discussion are not easy to define and are frequently defined differently by different participants in the discussion.[1] Technology may be defined very broadly (for example, as "knowledge of how to do all those things associated with economic activity"[2]), or it may be defined much more specifically (for example, as "a collection of physical processes which transforms inputs into outputs, together with the social arrangements—that is, organizational modes and procedural methods—which structure the activities involved in carrying out these transformations"[3]). What these and other definitions have in common, however, is the idea that technology is much more than a collection of blueprints, machinery, and equipment. By the same token, technology transfer is a much more complex affair than the shipment of objects from one country to another. Capital goods may be physically transferred, but they represent only part of the technology transfer process; the all-important element is the know-how that will enable the recipient to use those physical objects effectively.

Moreoever, what is transferred and the way in which it is transferred may be very different in the case of transfers between developed countries and those from developed to developing countries.[4] This is because the crucial ingredient in any transfer—know-how—can be more precisely defined and, in general, more easily accomplished when the transfer takes place between countries at approximately similar levels of technological development and with broadly similar endowments of the skills and technical infrastructure necessary to support the technology. In such a situation, the transfer itself may be made in a relatively codified form (for example, blueprints and formulas) and the recipient may be able to master the technology (that is, to use the transferred knowledge in an effective way) with relative ease.[5] Under these circumstances, only what is known as "core technology," elements of know-how related to the central process owned by the supplier, will generally need to be transferred.

By contrast, transfers between a developed and a developing country typically involve bridging a considerable "technological distance" because the recipient's level of technological development is much lower than the donor's.[6] This type of transfer has been defined as "the transfer of those elements of technical knowledge which are normally required in setting up and operating new production facilities or in extending existing ones—and which are characteristically in very short supply (and often totally absent) in developing countries."[7] These elements of technical knowledge may include what is known as "peripheral technology" in addition to core technology. The distinction between the two is illustrated in the next subsection.

Elements of a Technology Transfer

The technical expertise required to realize a hypothetical project from its conception to the point at which it is ready to start operation includes the ability to undertake the following:[8]

a. Preinvestment, feasibility, and marketing studies
b. Detailed preproject studies of alternative technologies which might be used in the project
c. Basic engineering—the embodiment of the central process chosen for the project into project-specific flow-sheets, layouts, and designs
d. Detailed engineering—architectural and construction plans for the plant, precise specifications of equipment and materials, installation plans, and so on
e. Procurement and construction
f. Training of project staff
g. Start-up and initial troubleshooting services.

These items correspond to the elements of technical knowledge referred to above. Only items c, f, and g represent the core technology that the supplier must provide—and would be likely to provide in a transfer between developed countries. The other components are examples of peripheral technology, which is not specific to a particular project or process, but is necessary for the realization of any manufacturing project. Technology of this type is generally available in developed countries but may be unavailable in developing countries to a varying degree, depending on their levels of technological sophistication.

In addition to the items listed above, the recipient needs various kinds of expertise to run the project after start-up. They include management, marketing, maintenance, and quality control services. Again, some or all of these items may be unavailable within the recipient entity. Depending on the particular circumstances and the objectives of the supplier and recipient, a contract to supply a given technology may call for the supplier to provide some or all of these post-start-up items as well as some or all of the pre-start-up items listed above.

Direct versus Indirect Transfer and the Concept of Packaging

Potential recipients of core technology in a developing country may have all the elements required for project realization and operation, other than the core technology, available within their own organization. In some cases, however, only some (or none) of the elements may be available within the organization, but some or all of those lacking may be obtained locally or from entities in developed countries. In such cases there is a choice: the recipients can shop around locally or abroad for individual items or they can sign a more or less comprehensive contract with the owner of the core technology (or an intermediary) for the provision of some or all of the peripheral technology as well. The former process has been termed direct transfer of technology, and the latter called indirect transfer.[9] In the former case, the project promoter deals directly with the potential suppliers of individual elements; in the latter case, he has only indirect contact with them and leaves the owner of the core technology or a third-party contractor to supply or subcontract for peripheral items.

The more components the technology owner or a third party provides, other than the core technology, the more "packaged" a project is said to be. Many academic writers and commentators at policymaking levels in developing countries oppose the wholesale use of highly packaged transfers. They argue that packaging can cause the recipients to pay more than they need to for the items in the package; that unless special arrangements are made, such as seconding staff from the recipient entity to the supplier during implementation, packaging can limit the recipients' opportunities for learning-by-doing, which is generally considered to be central to the process of technological development;[10] and that, if the recipients do not themselves have the capacity to undertake the activities in the package, they should contract for them directly with local firms as far as possible, rather than bring them in en bloc from abroad.

In practice, however, especially in technically complex industries such as petrochemicals, most transfer contracts tend to be packaged to a greater or lesser degree. For the most sophisticated developing countries, the need to contract for all-embracing packages may diminish over time; nevertheless, even when many of the elements required for project realization are available locally, recipients may choose a relatively highly packaged form of transfer. This is not necessarily a result of supplier pressure. Recipients may choose a package provided by a foreign supplier, despite the local availability of some of its components, for several reasons. They may believe (correctly or incorrectly) that foreign suppliers of the peripheral technology are more efficient and reliable than local ones. They may be unwilling or unable (because of a lack of knowledge or contracting experience) to undertake the demanding task of soliciting, evaluating, and negotiating contracts directly with a host of individual suppliers of different components. They may expect that with a packaged contract project design and construction will be coordinated on the basis of an integrated timetable, physical components such as machinery will meet the exact specifications required by the core technology supplier,[11] and time otherwise spent by government officials and recipient entity managers in negotiating with several suppliers will be saved and transaction costs thus reduced.

Licensors also have strong motives for preferring packaging. In process industries such as petrochemicals, licensors fall into two broad categories: producers of the product whose process technology they are proposing to transfer (in the case of petrochemicals, chemical and oil companies), and nonproducers who own or are licensed to transfer processes but do not themselves manufacture petrochemicals (process developers and specialized engineering firms). The latter groups in particular, whose "product" is their know-how, want to maximize their profits by selling as many as possible of the pre-start-up elements of technical knowledge to the recipient. The producers may also prefer a package of pre-start-up services (which they may undertake themselves or contract out to engineering firms) because they consider it more likely that the project will then meet their specifications and be completed in a timely fashion.

The two licensor groups differ, however, in the degree of their poststart-up involvement with the recipient entity once the plant has become operational. Engineering companies and process developers are not usually interested in participating in the operational phase of the project, although they may want to be involved in any work to modify or scale up the original plant. Licensors who are also producers are in a different position; they may have a strong interest in ensuring that the new production unit is integrated into (or at least does not disrupt) their own global or regional production and marketing strategies. They will therefore frequently offer assistance with management and marketing, for example, in exchange for some kind of ownership position in the recipient entity. If the recipients are relatively inexperienced, they may consider an arrangement of this kind to be in their interest as well. They may take the same view about technology-sharing or grant-back arrangements, whereby each party agrees to inform the other of any new developments in technology; the licensor is assured that the recipients will not steal a march on him, and the recipients see themselves as able to take advantage of any improvements in the technology made by the licensor or other recipients with whom the licensor has similar arrangements.

The topics discussed here are at the heart of chapter 2, which draws on existing literature and empirical data specially collected for this study to describe the main participants on the supply side of petrochemical technology transfers to Latin America and licensors' motivations and preferred contractual arrangements. The thrust of the argument is that the different objectives of the two licensor groups (producers and nonproducers) lead them to prefer particular types of contractual arrangements—which may in turn affect the opportunities for indigenous technological development in the petrochemical industries of developing countries or the ownership structure of those industries. As already noted, however, we do not attempt to prove or disprove these theses, but rather confine ourselves to using verifiable data to show how participants' interests lead to certain types of transfer arrangements that include highly packaged pre-start-up services, licensor shareholdings, or other involvement in post-start-up operations. Before turning to these issues, however, we discuss two more general questions in the next two subsections.

Externalities and Social versus Private Costs

As noted above, the use of packaged transfer mechanisms is often perceived by recipients to offer (and may in fact provide) advantages to them. Even when these advantages are real and genuinely reduce the costs to the recipient of realizing or operating the project, it can nevertheless be argued that relatively unpackaged transfers offer opportunities for external benefits to the recipient country's economy—and that highly packaged transfers impose social costs on the economy which may outweigh their private benefits to the recipient entity. Protagonists of this position point out that packaged transfers may entail losses to *other* firms in the recipient's country, firms which could otherwise subcontract for civil engineering, equipment procurement, and (if the economy is relatively sophisticated) such pre-start-up activities as preliminary and pre-project studies or elements of detailed or basic process engineering. Even if local subcontractors are slower or less efficient than foreign ones, the use of foreign suppliers could impose a social cost on the recipient country's economy greater than the private benefits the technology recipient derives from using them. Because the potential benefits of using local firms are external to the recipient, they tend to be ignored in transfer transactions between developed country suppliers and developing country recipients—even when the latter are parastatal or government-owned entities.

The critical argument against highly packaged transfers, however, is that technological advance is based on learning-by-doing. The more packaged the project, the fewer the opportunities for indigenous learning-by-doing by both the recipient and potential local subcontractors. If the licensor who supplies a packaged transfer is a process developer or an engineering firm, the lost opportunities are likely to be mainly in the area of pre-start-up activities since the supplier provides some or all of the peripheral technology. If the supplier is a producer, the losses are likely to extend to post-start-up operations such as management and marketing. For example, in cases where suppliers contract to maintain the plant and equipment or provide modification services, the recipients and any specialized local groups which might perform these services lose the opportunity to develop skill in project management or design technology.[12]

Some opponents of packaged transfers suggest that the term "transfer of technology" may often be a misnomer. In many cases, technology (know-how) may be provided by the supplier, but only the first element of the triad of operational, project management, and project design technology is actually transferred to the recipient, in the sense that the recipient learns to master it. This form of transfer is sometimes described as "transfer of industry" rather than transfer of technology.

In recent years, some developing countries have legislated to limit or bar certain features of indirect or packaged transfer agreements.[13] Others have actively encouraged the use of local contractors or have set up state enterprises to carry out activities associated with peripheral and even core technology. (These and other matters relating to recipient countries and entities will be discussed in some detail in chapter 3, which deals with local petrochemical markets, government policies toward foreign investment and technology transfer, the participants in local petrochemical industries, and levels of local technical expertise.)

Critics of these initiatives point to the danger of misallocating resources by supporting local enterprises which may be inefficient. They also suggest that recipients are often quite content to negotiate packaged transfers, as noted above. Finally, they contend that suppliers might retaliate by refusing to transfer technology if recipient countries' policies in this area become too restrictive. The first of these three issues is well known, of wide general application, and not specifically related to technology transfer; it is not discussed further here. The second and the third issues are referred to in later chapters in the light of available empirical evidence.

One additional general issue relating to externalities needs to be addressed. It can be argued that, although the benefits of using indigenous contractors may be wholly or partially external to the recipient entity, they are *internal* to other local enterprises. Consequently, local engineering firms, for example, should invest in their own future by competing with foreign contractors at rock-bottom prices in order to gain contracts and the learning experience they offer. This argument may have some theoretical merit, but it ignores some important practical problems of an institutional kind: (a) recipient entities, rightly or wrongly, tend to choose foreign subcontractors over local ones even when the latter have a clear price advantage, because they believe that the superior expertise of the foreign firms offers better prospects for the timely and technically sound completion of the project; (b) technology owners tend to offer performance guarantees only if engineering contractors with an established track record in the field are used; and (c) financing agencies (both official and private) tend to make funding conditional on the employment of established international contractors. As will be shown in chapter 3, these problems are not insurmountable; local entities do in fact obtain procurement and engineering contracts. It would be unduly simplistic, however, to assume that competition from local firms based on price alone can overcome the technical and institutional factors favoring packaged technology transfers.

Two Theories of Technology Transfer

As noted earlier, licensors who supply technology in process industries such as petrochemicals can be divided into two groups: technology owners who are themselves producers, and process developers and engineering firms who may own or contract to supply processes but do not themselves engage in production. The latter's "products" are core processes and associated peripheral technology; their motive in selling technology is therefore quite straightforward. The case of process owners who are also themselves producers is less simple: why would a producer export his technology, rather than his product, to recipient countries?

Several specific factors may encourage producers to license a process or to invest in a plant overseas. These include the desire to take advantage of local outlets in recipient countries or to set up foreign subsidiaries so as to preserve a global or regional monopoly; the need to overcome tariff or nontariff barriers imposed by recipient countries on imports of the product concerned; and perhaps, in the case of petrochemicals, home country restrictions on the expansion of polluting industries or the need to locate plants so as to ensure adequate supplies of raw materials (oil and gas).

On a more general level, economists have developed two so-called neotechnology theories to explain the international diffusion of production technology. One is based on the idea of a technology gap, the other on the life cycle of a product.

TECHNOLOGY GAP THEORY. The first theory suggests that technology is diffused according to the following sequence of events:

- Competitive pressure in advanced economies causes innovators to develop new products or more efficient processes for producing existing ones.
- The innovator is then in a quasi-monopolistic position and will supply foreign markets by exporting; these exports are called "technology gap trade" because they are based on a technological advantage over all other producers.

- In time, however, competitors in other countries will succeed in imitating the innovator's technology. The period between first production by an innovator and first production by an imitator is called the imitation lag; with imitation, "technology gap trade" will decline.
- Once production spreads to low-wage developing countries, the flow of trade will reverse, because producers in these countries will have significant cost advantages over those in high-wage advanced countries.

Empirical studies of synthetics and plastics have produced only limited evidence in support of the technology gap theory.[14] In the case of synthetics, the first stage of the theory appeared to hold, but the reverse flow of exports did not occur—probably because wages represented a small proportion of total costs, and the benefits of production in a low-wage country were therefore insignificant. In plastics, it appeared that although the innovator's advantage in terms of costs and prices for standard materials was reduced over time, his opportunities for research and development enabled him to retain some degree of lasting leadership through improvements in product quality.

Nevertheless, in view of the increasingly similar technical capabilities of the leading petrochemical producers and the consequences of developing countries' import substitution policies, producers may wish to license their products relatively quickly to entities in developing countries. In fact, there is evidence that this process is occurring at an accelerating rate. Analyses carried out for this book show that the mean lag in years between the first use of petrochemical technology in the world and its first use in Latin America has consistently grown shorter for the more recent innovations. It took a mean of nearly 28 years for processes first developed in 1939 or earlier to be introduced into Latin America; processes developed between 1950 and 1959 were first used in Latin America after a mean lag of only 12 years; for processes developed since 1965, the mean lag fell to 7.3 years. In addition to the causal factors already noted, the growth of refining facilities has probably accelerated the transfer process in Latin America, since refinery by-products are used as raw materials for petrochemical production.

PRODUCT LIFE CYCLE THEORY. According to the technology gap theory, production processes spread from their country of origin as imitators in other countries become able to compete successfully with the original innovator. By contrast, the product life cycle theory postulates that the location of production is determined less by the pressure of imitators in other countries than by the decision of the original innovator or early imitators to set up subsidiaries or affiliates overseas—at first in other developed countries and eventually in countries in the developing world.[15] Innovation and production in the initial stage of a product's life cycle will take place in a country with a large internal market and high per capita income. The product and its associated processes will not be standardized at this stage; the manufacturer will locate the productive facilities close to prospective buyers in order to facilitate communication and will adapt the product's specifications to the buyers' requirements. Strong product differentiation at this stage will mean that comparative cost factors are of relatively little importance.

As demand expands over time, the product and its production processes are likely to become more standardized. Opportunities for mass production emerge, costs become a more important factor, and it becomes worthwhile to consider setting up production facilities abroad. The theory suggests that the factors encouraging such a move include lower labor costs or locational advantages of other kinds; the threat of competition in other countries from local or other foreign producers of the now-standardized product; and the fact that, once an investment has been made in learning about customers' needs in a particular overseas market and in setting up a sales and servicing network, the marginal cost of building a production plant to serve that market is considerably reduced. Plants will be built initially in other developed countries and possibly eventually in developing countries.

The theory also suggests that, *within* the overseas expansion phase, licensors of technologies will choose different types of overseas operation over time, in response to the gradual erosion of their monopolistic advantage. Initially, while their products are still relatively new and strongly differentiated, licensors will opt for wholly owned subsidiaries; later they choose joint ventures, and finally licensing arrangements that may include contractual restrictions on the licensee's operations but need not involve supplier equity participation.

The product life cycle theory has been tested empirically in a number of studies. One of these used the theory to explain the location of investment for nine intermediate petrochemical products.[16] The study (which covered 360 plants, 44 of which were in developing countries) found that as predicted by the theory, the first commercialization of products occurred in countries which had large domestic markets. Also as expected, the number of producers increased with increasing standardization over the products' life cycles. Contrary to expectations, exports did not fall over time to the extent that the theory suggested.

Overall foreign control over facilities in recipient countries fell over time, in part because of the increasing role in the transfer process of nonproducing imitators (that is, engineering firms), which, as noted earlier, rarely participate in recipients' post-start-up activities. The stages of the life cycle did not, however, significantly affect the choice of contractual arrangements (subsidiaries versus joint ventures with entities in recipient countries) when the supplier of production technology was a producer. In fact, facilities set up by producers at *later* stages of the products' life cycles were *more* likely to be wholly owned subsidiaries than ones built in earlier stages. It appeared that the size of the producer firm and its basic product orientation were the main variables determining the type of contractual arrangements used. Because larger firms were able to accept a higher degree of risk—and were probably able to attract more risk capital—they were more likely than smaller ones to set up wholly owned subsidiaries. Furthermore, chemical companies were more likely than oil companies to set up subsidiaries—probably because the former were inclined to view overseas production as part of their overall international production and marketing effort, while the latter viewed foreign licensees of petrochemicals as outlets for feedstocks rather than part of their core operations, and were therefore less concerned about owning the recipient entity outright.

Other findings of this study suggested that investment outside the United States was initially concentrated in large markets; that a good investment climate and relatively great distance from major producing countries significantly shortened the lag between first commercialization and overseas production; and that, as noted above, the entry of nonproducing imitators into the market as a product matured led to a marked rise in licensing agreements as opposed to agreements involving supplier participation in a recipient's equity. Other factors such as tariff barriers, a country's level of development, and, most important, wage rates did not appear to affect location or the lag between first commercialization and overseas production.

These findings relate mainly to how technology transfers take place between developed countries, which account for 87 percent of the sample of firms used as empirical evidence for the study. In cases of this kind, suppliers and recipients are at similar levels of technological development and government intervention in the transfer process is very limited. The focus of the present study is different in that it concentrates exclusively on the transfer of petrochemical technology between developed and developing countries. In transfers of this kind, conditions in the developing country, such as its level of technological development and the nature and extent of government intervention, can be more important determinants of transfer mechanisms than the stage reached by the product in its life cycle. In addition, our sample is not limited to intermediate products; it also covers basic and final products. These three product groups tend to be transferred under different types of arrangements, because the technology suppliers (producers or nonproducers) for each group tend to have different market objectives and may be subject to different kinds of government regulations in recipient countries.

A further difference between our study and the one discussed above lies in the definition of maturity. While the earlier study uses the long-term growth rates of consumption of a particular product in the U.S. market to determine its stage in the product cycle, we define maturity in terms of the age of the product or the process used to produce it, or the gap, in years, between first use of the product or process in the world and first use in the recipient country.

Later in the present study, detailed empirical evidence will be presented that relates to the relevance of maturity factors to the process of petrochemical technology transfers between developed and developing countries. At this stage, it is worth noting a number of general points which suggest that its applicability to petrochemicals may be (at best) limited:

• The theory assumes that technology becomes more standardized with product maturity. In petrochemicals, however, *process innovation* may continue throughout a product's life cycle, even after the product itself has become standardized, and *final products* may not become standardized over time because they may change their characteristics quite frequently in response to user demand.

• The theory assumes that nonproducing imitators should be mainly providers of standardized, mature technology. This is by no means necessarily the case in petrochemicals, because specialization in the industry is based on type of product (final, intermediate, or basic) rather than on maturity—that is, some processes are typically supplied by producers and some by nonproducers. This point is discussed further in chapter 2.

• The original statement of the theory noted that the goods for which production in developing countries would be appropriate would be those with significant labor inputs. In the case of petrochemicals, however, labor costs are a relatively insignificant factor in overall production costs. This is especially true for basic and intermediate products, which are generally manufactured in very large and capital-intensive plants. Other reasons, such as recipient countries' import substitution policies and distance from producers, the size of their markets, and the availability of raw materials, may help explain the location of petrochemical plants in developing countries—but these factors may make investment in developing countries attractive to process owners regardless of product maturity.

• The theory suggests that, as a product matures, the typical contractual arrangements for transfer change from an initial emphasis on wholly owned subsidiaries to joint ventures and then to licensing agreements. Empirical evidence shows, however, that the pattern of contractual arrangements in petrochemicals is by no means so clear-cut. This point is discussed further in chapter 2; empirical data on the relationship between product maturity and different types of contractual arrangements are presented in chapter 4.

Summary and Conclusion

Some of the general concepts associated with technology transfer have been presented here as background for the more detailed discussions in chapters 2 and 3 of suppliers' and recipients' behavior. In the process we have begun to define in general terms what it is that is transferred and why transfers take place. It has been suggested that know-how is a crucial element in technology and in "genuine" transfers of technology (as opposed to transfers of industry); that the transfer of know-how from a developed to a developing country is much more difficult than from one developed country to another, because of the technological distance between supplier and recipient; that packaged transfers, involving the provision (but not necessarily transfer in a real sense) of project design and management technology, are often perceived by recipients as well as suppliers to be in their private interest, but that such transactions may have social costs, especially by inhibiting indigenous technological development through local learning-by-doing; and, finally, that the two main neotechnology theories of technology transfer may well have only limited application to the transfers of petrochemical technology between developed and developing countries. Some of these propositions will be examined in detail, in the special context of such transfers to Latin America, in chapters 2 and 3.

Notes

1. Charles M. Cooper and Francisco Sercovitch, *The Channels and Mechanisms for the Transfer of Technology from Developed to Developing Countries*, TR/B/AC 11/5 (Geneva: UNCTAD, April 1971); and Organisation for Economic Co-operation and Development, *North-South Technology Transfer: The Way Ahead* (Paris: OECD, 1981).

2. Frances Stewart, *International Technology Transfer: Issues and Policy Options*, World Bank Staff Working Paper no. 344 (Washington, D.C., 1979).

3. Carl J. Dahlman and Larry E. Westphal, "The Meaning of Technological Mastery in Relation to Transfer of Technology," *Annals of the American Academy of Political and Social Science*, vol. 458 (Fall 1981).

4. Rachel McCulloch, "Technology Transfer to Developing Countries: Implications of International Regulation," *Annals of the American Academy of Political and Social Science*, vol. 458 (Fall 1981).

5. David J. Teece, "The Market for Know-How and the Efficient International Transfer of Technology," *Annals of the American Academy of Political and Social Science*, vol. 458 (Fall 1981); Dahlman and Westphal, "The Meaning of Technological Mastery."

6. OECD, *North-South Technology Transfer*.

7. Cooper and Sercovitch, *Channels and Mechanisms for the Transfer of Technology*.

8. The listing used here is an amalgamation and simplification of the categories used in Cooper and Sercovitch, *Channels and Mechanisms for the Transfer of Technology*, and Dahlman and Westphal, "The Meaning of Technological Mastery."

9. Cooper and Sercovitch, *Channels and Mechanisms for the Transfer of Technology*.

10. Charles M. Cooper, *Policy Interventions for Technological Innovation in Developing Countries*, World Bank Staff Working Paper no. 441 (Washington, D.C., 1980).

11. Teece, "The Market for Know-How."

12. Stewart, "International Technology Transfer"; Dahlman and Westphal, "The Meaning of Technological Mastery."

13. United Nations, "The Acquisition of Technology from Multinational Corporations by Developing Countries," E.74.II.A.7 (New York, 1974).

14. C. G. Hufbauer, *Synthetic Materials and the Theory of International Trade* (Cambridge, Mass.: Harvard University Press, 1966); C. Freeman, "The Plastics Industry: A Comparative Study of Research and Innovation," *National Institute Economic Review*, no. 26 (November 1963).

15. Raymond Vernon, "International Investment and International Trade in the Product Cycle," *Quarterly Journal of Economics*, vol. 80, no. 1 (May 1966).

16. R. B. Stobaugh, "The Product Life Cycle, U.S. Exports and International Investment," D.B.A. dissertation, Harvard University Graduate School of Business Administration, 1968.

Chapter 2

Petrochemical Technology Transfer: The Suppliers

The remainder of this book is devoted to a relatively detailed examination of North-South transfers to a particular region—Latin America—and within a particular industry—petrochemicals. Although the treatment is necessarily simplified and the petrochemical industry and the Latin American market for its technology exhibit some special features, the picture presented has implications for the broader debate about the terms and conditions of technology transfers between powerful, often multinational corporations based in the industrialized North and recipient entities in the industrializing South. This chapter deals with the suppliers of petrochemical technology to Latin America.

Participants on the Supply Side

The most important supplier group comprises the owners of core technology—North American, European, and Japanese firms which sell their processes in the Latin America market. Other supply side participants, however, can and do influence the terms and conditions under which technology is transferred—either through their participation in a packaged transfer negotiated by a process owner or through agreements they may independently make with recipients to provide inputs other than core technology needed for project implementation. This discussion begins by introducing the suppliers of core technology (process owners) and then turns to the suppliers of the peripheral technology and investment funds needed by petrochemical plants in Latin America (contractors, equipment suppliers, and financing agencies).

Process Owners

As noted in chapter 1, process owners can be divided for analytical purposes into two broad categories—those who are also producers (chemical and oil companies) and those who are not (specialized process developers and engineering firms). This bifurcation of the supply side of the market reflects the growing specialization of function in the industry—which is in turn a consequence of the increasing scale and complexity of petrochemical production systems. The development of an autonomous engineering function, separate from production, is common among industries characterized by heavy investment requirements, complex technologies, and the need to make large numbers of project-specific adaptations to the core processes used. In addition to petrochemicals, industries of this kind include steel, nonferrous metals, power generation, mining, and continuous-process industries such as oil, chemicals, and paper.[1]

Specialization by product type (basic, intermediate, and final) among process owners is marked in the petrochemical industry. The twenty-six products covered in the empirical research for this study are made up of five basic, fourteen intermediate, and seven final products. The three types of product are distinguished according to their position in the production chain. Basic products are derived directly from raw material in oil or natural gas streams; intermediates are manufactured from basics, and final products are made from intermediates (or basics). Table 2-1 shows the number of processes available for the manufacture of each product by type of process owner. Over half (56 percent) of the processes for basic products are owned by engineering firms or process developers, and another 8 percent of these processes are jointly owned by members of both groups; nearly three-quarters (72 percent) of the processes for intermediate products and nearly nine-tenths (89 percent) of those for final products are owned by producers.

The reasons for this pattern of ownership are straightforward. Final products tend to be nonstandardized, to be associated with specific brand names, and to require very heavy initial research and development expenditures, including pilot plant production. The scale of these expenditures can be illustrated very simply: in 1971 the chemical companies with the largest research and development outlays in the United States, Federal Republic of Germany, United Kingdom, and France spent the following amounts:

Dupont (United States): $250 million (6.4 percent of value of sales)
Bayer (Germany): $149 million (4.8 percent of value of sales)
Imperial Chemical Industries (ici, United Kingdom): $148 million (3.6 percent of value of sales)
Rhone-Poulenc (France): $100 million (4.3 percent of value of sales)

These very large expenditures have led to a concentration of product and initial process innovation in the hands of producer companies, as shown by the number of patents taken out by producers and nonproduc-

Table 2-1. *Processes Available for 26 Selected Petrochemical Products, 1963–73: 280 Petrochemical Plants*
(number)

				Processes owned		
Product	Process types	Processes available	Companies offering processes	By producers	By engineering firms and process developers	In collabo- ration
Basic						
Ethylene	3[a]	23	21	6	17	0
Benzene	6[b]	28	22	10	12	6
Butadiene	4	16	12	11	4	1
Ammonia	4[c]	27	17	7	19	1
Methanol	2[c]	21	16	8	12	1
Intermediate						
Acetaldehyde	4	6	6	6	0	0
Acrylonitrile	3	10	11	8	2	0
Caprolactam	4	13	12	11	2	0
Cyclohexane	1	15	16	8	6	1
Dimethyl terephthalate and terephthalic acid	4	20	20	15	4	1

Dodecylbenzene	1	7	7	6	1	0
Ethylene oxide	1	12	10	9	3	0
Formaldehyde	3	18	17	13	4	1
Phenol	9	17	16	11	5	1
Phthalic anhydride	3	21	20	16	5	0
Isopropanol	3	9	10	8	1	0
Styrene	1	13	15	8	3	2
Vinyl chloride monomer	6	34	31	26	6	2
Urea	1	12	12	3	7	2
Final						
Low-density polyethylene	1	22	22	19	3	0
High-density polyethylene	1	19	20	17	2	0
Polystyrene	3	24	25	19	4	1
Polyvinyl chloride	2	28	30	25	3	0
Styrene butadiene rubber	2	11	11	11	0	0
Polypropylene	1	10	10	10	0	0
Carbon black	1	7	7	7	0	0

a. We considered the steam pyrolysis of butane, ethane, gas oil, naphtha, and propane to be one type of process. They could be considered as different processes adapted to different feedstocks, in which case the number of processes would be seven.

b. Excluding catalytic reforming of naphtha and cracked gasoline hydrogenation.

c. The two processes are high-pressure and low-pressure synthesis. The synthesized gas can be made by direct oxidation or steam reforming and the feedstock can be naphtha, liquefied petroleum gas, natural gas, or a mixture of carbon monoxide and hydrogen.

ers respectively. For example, Dupont registered more than 3,000 patents with the U.S. Department of Commerce between 1969 and 1973; ici registered very nearly the same number in London between 1959 and 1966. By comparison, the largest number of London patent registrations by an engineering firm during the same period was 246, by Lurgi of Germany; the U.S. and U.K. contractors with the largest number of patents were respectively Foster Wheeler with 108 and Simon Carves with 106.

In general, final products tend to be manufactured on a relatively small scale compared with intermediate and especially with basic products. (Data on Latin American plant capacities by country and product group are presented in appendix A.) In the few cases where process developers or engineering firms own technologies for final products, the technology is usually widely diffused and the products are manufactured in large quantities.

Widely diffused technology and large-scale production are the rule rather than the exception at the other end of the production chain. Basic petrochemicals are generic, and the processes used to manufacture them are generally simple, widely known, and practically unprotected by patents. They also tend to be manufactured in petrochemical complexes with high production capacities. The problems associated with setting up plants to produce basic petrochemicals thus normally relate less to the acquisition of the core technology than to the extreme complexity of the process engineering requirements. Process developers and engineering firms, which specialize in scaling up production processes and designing appropriate manufacturing facilities, consequently predominate in this subsector of the market.

The mixed picture of process ownership presented by intermediate products reflects the broad pattern of specialization of function on the part of producers and nonproducers outlined above. In the case of products characterized by high output volumes and widely diffused technologies, engineering firms and process developers are likely to own some of the available production processes. Nevertheless, producers own the majority of processes in this subsector; their dominance is particularly marked in the case of intermediates which are produced by fairly sophisticated processes and which have been developed in association with the final products for which they are inputs.

As will be demonstrated empirically in later sections, the pattern of ownership is not necessarily carried over into the pattern of transfers. In some cases, favorable local market conditions may make it attractive for a producer firm to set up a local subsidiary using a technology owned by a nonproducer (an engineering firm or process developer). In other cases, a producer will not itself act as supplier for a process it owns, but will use an engineering firm as a transfer agent. The agent may have financial links with the producer or may be an independent entity which has participated in the development or scaling up of a given process.[2] Producers may also license more than one engineering firm as transfer agent for processes they own. The choice of agent is generally made on the basis of previous cooperation or the size and proven commercial and technical capability of the engineering firms concerned.[3]

Producers tend to favor the use of engineering firms as transfer agents when it proves necessary to analyze and adapt laboratory or pilot plant work to tailor the process design to the specialized needs of a potential recipient. If the demand for a particular process is large enough, however, the producer's own engineering department will prepare process designs.

COMPETITIVENESS AMONG PROCESS OWNERS. Analysis of the data in table 2-1 suggests that a variety of companies supply the processes for most of the products listed. On the basis of the figures in the table, it appears that an average of 16 suppliers exists for each product, ranging from a minimum of six firms offering a process for producing acetaldehyde to a maximum of 31 offering a process for vinyl chloride monomer. These figures are somewhat misleading, however, since different processes use different inputs and have different by-products; consequently a potential recipient may be more restricted in his choice than the table suggests. Moreover, as noted in chapter 1, both producer and nonproducer owners of core technology are likely to want to negotiate packaged contracts in which conditions of one kind or another are attached to transfers. For example, producers may wish to specify the engineering firm for pre-start-up work on the project (if they do not wish to undertake this work themselves) or to take an ownership position in the recipient entity; even if the producer grants a license without equity participation, he may wish to include conditions in the contract about post-start-up matters such as marketing and technology sharing. Nonproducer owners of core technology, by contrast, being in the business of selling technical services, will wish to strike a bargain which allows them to undertake or subcontract as many as possible of the elements of peripheral technology needed in a new project's pre-start-up phase.

Nevertheless, a degree of competition does exist among the members of each group of process owners—and to some extent, in the area of process innovation, between members of the two groups. As noted, the position of an innovator can quickly be eroded because his competitors are increasingly likely to have technical expertise similar to his own. For the industry as a whole, although the rate at which fundamental break-throughs occur seems to be slowing down, the diffusion of existing technologies and the development of close substitutes for existing products seem to be accelerating. Moreover, process innovation, such as using alternative inputs or jumping a stage in the production chain, is a feature of the industry. This means that a firm can become a market leader even after the product has become fully standardized (see the critique of the product life cycle theory in chapter 1); through process innovation, a nonproducer can overtake a producer or vice versa.

The perceived likelihood of competitive pressure can lead process owners to license their processes as quickly as possible, before others compete away their temporary advantage. Both the extent to which process innovation can affect costs and the innovator's willingness to license a new process quickly (rather than attempting to capitalize on the innovation by retaining a monopoly of its use) are illustrated by Sohio's development of the ammonoxidization process for the production of acrylonitrile in 1960. The new process reduced prices from a historic high of US $0.38 to US $0.12 a pound in 1973. By that year, Sohio had supplied the technology to thirty-five plants; the first license for the process was granted to Asahi in Japan only two years after its first use in the United States.

Sometimes, however, a particular process can have characteristics which give it and its owner a lasting advantage over all potential competitors. For example, a German company, Aldehyde, developed two processes for the oxidization of ethylene to acetaldehyde in 1960. Thirteen years later, although six other processes were available, all six acetaldehyde plants in Latin America used Aldehyde's process. The case of the Von Hayden process for the production of phthalic anhydride is similar; despite the existence of twenty similar processes, more than sixty-five plants throughout the world used this process in 1973, including six of the twelve phthalic anhydride plants in Latin America.

SUMMARY AND CONCLUSION. This subsection has briefly sketched the main characteristics of the central entities on the supply side of the petrochemical technology transfer process. It has shown that the market is bifurcated, with two groups—producers and nonproducers—transferring core technology. These groups have different objectives when they make transfers, and appear to specialize in different sectors of the market (this proposition will be examined further in the light of detailed empirical evidence).

Although a large number of process owners offer technology for the manufacture of each of the twenty-six products surveyed for this study, the apparent competitiveness of the market is limited by factors related to the characteristics of individual processes. Another limitation is that process owners, whether producers or nonproducers, tend to attach conditions—though of different types—to transfer agreements. Nevertheless, with a few notable exceptions, the close similarity of their competitors' technical capabilities makes it difficult for innovators to dominate the market for a particular process indefinitely.

Producer and nonproducer owners of core technology are not, however, the only participants on the supply side of the petrochemical technology transfer market. The next subsection briefly discusses some other major participants and explores some of the linkages among them and between them and process owners.

Other Supply Side Participants

As has already been noted, a technological distance typically exists between a developed country supplier of a core technology and its recipient in a developing country. As a result, recipients frequently have to rely on external entities (generally based in developed countries) for the peripheral technology needed to realize a project. They are also likely to need more money than they can generate from their own resources— especially in an industry such as petrochemicals, in which new plants typically have heavy initial investment costs. Three groups, other than core process owners, are most frequently involved in transfers of petrochemical technology to Latin America: engineering contractors, equipment suppliers, and financing agencies.

ENGINEERING CONTRACTORS. As noted above, engineering firms may transfer core process technologies that they themselves own, or act as transfer agents of core technology owned by producer firms. Engineering firms may also act as contractors to supply some or all of the elements of peripheral technology when core technology is transferred by its owner. We have already outlined the role and objectives of the engineering firm as the supplier of core technology; this subsection is mainly concerned with its role as contractor for peripheral technology.

Engineering contractors vary widely in the services they offer. At one end of the scale are a small number of multinational general contracting firms which are capable of organizing all aspects of a project (including financing);[4] at the other end are small engineering consultancy groups (including local firms in developing countries), which may be able to undertake only preliminary or pre-project studies, or may carry out all peripheral technology services including detailed engineering. In some cases, contractors may be subsidiaries of process owners or of industrial or financial groups.[5]

Not all engineering contractors are based in developed countries. As will be illustrated in detail in chapter 3, several countries in Latin America have developed different degrees of indigenous project engineering expertise. In some cases, local contractors can provide services comparable to those offered by foreign groups and at less cost because of their lower charges per engineering hour; moreover, their familiarity with local conditions may give them an advantage over outsiders.

Petrochemical engineering contracting services are subject to strong cyclical variations in demand. Contractors generally prefer to charge on the basis of a fixed fee for head office costs plus hourly charges for engineering services, with additional charges for costs of materials, equipment, and construction work if applicable. If demand is low, however, contractors may be willing to accept a straight fixed price contract (even if the margin of profit is low) to cover the costs of maintaining their staffs. Thus, the engineering costs of a project may vary considerably, depending on the point in the cycle at which a contract is signed.

Latin America has for some time been an important market for international chemical plant contractors, ranking second only to Western Europe in the value (about $1,800 million) of contracts signed with foreign contractors in 1970. In that year, over 80 percent of such contracts were with U.S. firms; by 1973, the U.S. share had fallen to just over 60 percent, with European contractors (notably firms based in the Federal Republic of Germany, France, and Italy) gaining sharply. In more recent years, the dollar value of contracts between foreign firms and entities in Latin America has remained roughly stable at about $1,800 million a year; the relative importance of the Latin American market has declined, however, owing to rapid increases in demand in the Middle East.

EQUIPMENT SUPPLIERS. Much of the equipment used in petrochemical plants is fairly standardized. Some items of equipment that have been developed along with the process itself, however, must be supplied by the owner of the technology or by specialized fabricators. These items include special compressors, furnaces, turbines, various types of pumps, electronics, and instrumentation.

Recipient countries themselves produce much of the standardized equipment used in their plants, although the percentage of locally supplied equipment varies with the level of indigenous technological expertise (for examples, see chapter 3). Most specialized equipment is, however, supplied by independent component makers, working closely with engineering and chemical firms, which are the main sources of new component requirements. Component makers usually adapt their production to the specifications supplied by process owners, but some of them are strong enough in research and development to initiate and diffuse process innovations themselves; for example, APV Company Ltd. has pioneered several successful innovations. In addition, some chemical and engineering firms have their own fabricating facilities. This is because, until recently, chemical firms often had to design and manufacture critical components themselves since equipment suppliers could not, or would not, work to the exacting specifications required.

Japanese equipment suppliers represent something of a special case. They are usually part of broadly based organizations with extensive plant fabrication facilities, and they are consequently more interested than their U.S. or European counterparts in selling a package that includes both engineering services and equipment. In general, however, chemical firms do not favor links between engineering firms and equipment fabricators, believing that an independent engineering firm is more likely to choose equipment on the basis of its technical quality.

Although increasing specialization and division of labor have led to less involvement of chemical and engineering firms in equipment manufacturing, there is a predictably strong relationship between the country in which design engineering is done and the country in which hardware is procured.[6] This is so for several reasons. Contractors' design and procurement offices are most familiar with domestic suppliers of equipment and can inspect and oversee their output relatively easily. Moreover, financing agencies may often require that procurement take place in their national markets.[7] Finally, the process chosen by the client and contractor is often based on one originally developed and used in the contractor's country of origin; there is therefore a tendency to use components and specifications from that country.

FINANCING AGENCIES. The petrochemical industry is capital intensive and subject to large economies of scale; plants consequently require large amounts of both initial investment and working capital. State ownership and financing of plants to manufacture basic and intermediate products are quite common in developing countries, in part because governments have access to international sources of long-term borrowing and nonequity capital. By contrast, private firms in developing countries are usually unable to tap these sources unless they have foreign participation in their equity or are guaranteed by their governments.

The availability of funds from foreign banks and international agencies for equity or debt financing is usually conditional on the participation of the technology supplier as an equity shareholder and partner in the post-start-up stage of the project, because their presence is perceived as a guarantee of the success of the new venture. These sources of financing can also influence the selection of engineering firms to organize the pre-start-up phase of the project as well as the terms of contracts with them and of the guarantees they provide.

Commercial banks are generally unwilling to finance plants unless the contractor is based in their own country (an attitude not limited to petrochemical projects). Banks may favor particular engineering firms or equipment suppliers because of the guarantees they offer or because they have special links with these firms. These links may be through direct ownership or less direct cooperative agreements to supply package deals, especially in overseas markets.[8] Most big commercial banks have their own technical engineering groups that identify potential sources of demand and provide information on technology. These groups permit banks to play an active role in organizing credits for a given project.

In addition, engineering firms and equipment suppliers may themselves provide funds in the form of suppliers' credits. This is done through lines of credit with banks of which they are clients or subsidiaries and, in some cases, through government guarantees of their overseas operations.

Finally, official agencies in developed countries may provide debt financing by guaranteeing export credits for the purchase of goods and services for industrial projects, as part of their export promotion policies. Governments may also subsidize rates of interest on project financing for the same reason.

Domestic financing agencies in developing countries cannot begin to match the array of financial resources which support overseas suppliers of know-how and equipment. Local banks in developing countries generally ration credit, do not usually lend for very large projects, and are rarely able to offer long-term loans or the grace periods typically needed for petrochemical projects. (Grace periods of up to three years are usually given by international banks.) Even if local banks have adequate financial resources, as may be the case in a country such as Venezuela (although even the Venezuelan government has had to obtain external credit to finance its industrial development program), it is not easy to transform money capital into long-term credit. Local banking structures are often inflexible, and banks lack the necessary connections with industrial concerns.

This situation has adverse implications for local engineering firms and equipment manufacturers. Nevertheless, some financial institutions, such as the Banco Econômico de Bahia and Banco Itau in Brazil, have financed local petrochemical projects by participating in the equity of the recipient firms. Local development corporations, such as Banco Nacional de Desenvolvimento Econômico in Brazil and Nacional Financiera in Mexico, have also provided financing for petrochemical projects, especially when state-owned petrochemical corporations are involved. In general, however, the close connections between financial institutions and industrial enterprises in developed countries, together with inadequate levels of savings (and therefore of dependable local sources of long-term finance) in developing countries, tend to encourage the transfer of technology in a highly packaged form by foreign suppliers. As a result, the opportunities for local engineering firms and equipment suppliers to participate in petrochemical projects in Latin America are often limited. (This issue is discussed in greater detail in chapter 3.)

Sources of Petrochemical Technology Transfers

This subsection presents detailed empirical evidence about the sources of transfers of core technology, whether undertaken by producers or nonproducers.

The specialization of ownership of technology by product type has already been noted. The logical supposition is that transfers will be specialized in the same way—that producers will be the main sources of technology transfers for final products, and that nonproducers will be the main sources of transfers for basic products. On the basis of the process ownership data provided at the beginning of this chapter, producers might be expected also to be the principal sources of production technology for intermediates. The fact that a company owns a process, however, does not mean that it will invariably be the transfer agent for its own core technology. Some processes may be owned by producers but widely licensed through engineering firms without any owner-imposed conditions about either pre- or post-start-up activities. In other cases, the producer may have an equity holding in the licensed engineering group and/or impose conditions on the transfer, such as equity participation in the recipient entity, limitations on plant size, or grant-back of technical improvements developed by the recipient.

For the purposes of this study, a situation of the first type—a transfer by an engineering company of a process owned by a producer who attaches no conditions to it—is counted as a nonproducer transfer, even though a producer is the original owner of the process being transferred; one of the second or third kind—a transfer of a producer-owned process, with an engineering company as transfer agent but with ultimate producer control over the technology and hence over the arrangements for transfer—is counted as a transfer by the producer, even though the transfer may be physically performed by a nonproducer.

The rationale for this treatment is that we are interested in examining whether control over a technology by one type of supplier or another (a producer or a nonproducer) significantly affects the terms and conditions under which the technology is transferred. In a situation of the first kind, the engineering firm is acting as a principal in the transaction; the absence of restrictions imposed by the original developer of the technology makes the engineering firm effectively its controller or "owner," and the contractual arrangements for transfer will reflect the engineering company's interests and concerns. In a situation of the second and third kinds, however, the engineering company is not a free agent; it is acting effectively as a subcontractor for the owner of the technology, and the contractual arrangements for transfer will reflect the controlling owner's interests and concerns.

The determinants of contractual arrangements for transfer will be discussed later. In this subsection we attempt to establish, with the use of empirical data specially collected for this study, what determines whether the principal participant on the supply side of petrochemical technology transfers (the effective source of the technology) is either a producer (a chemical or oil company) or a nonproducer (an engineering firm or process developer). Two kinds of possible determining factors are examined: the type of product for which the technology is transferred, and a range of factors related to product and process maturity.

TYPE OF PRODUCT. How closely is the pattern of technology *ownership* matched by the pattern of *transfer*? It will be recalled that ownership seemed to be strongly linked to type of product, with nonproducers owning 56 percent of the processes for basic products, and producers owning 72 percent of the processes for intermediates and 89 percent of the processes for final products.

Table 2-2 shows the sources of technology transfer for the 280 plants surveyed for this study. Taking the full seven-country sample of all 280 plants and excluding the unknowns, nonproducers were the sources of technology for 53 out of 65 plants making basic products, that is, for 82 percent of this subgroup. In the case of intermediate products, producers were the sources of technology for 51 plants out of 92 where the source was known, that is, for 55 percent of this subgroup. Producers were also the sources of technology for 62 plants out of 65 making final products where the source was known, that is, for 95 percent of this subsample.

Thus it appears that the pattern of transfers by product type broadly follows the pattern of ownership, although nonproducers' proportion of transfers was higher than their proportion of ownership in the cases of basic and intermediate products while producers' proportion of transfers was higher than their proportion of ownership in the case of final products. Statistical tests of the data showed that, for all countries, the likelihood of error in predicting the source of technology was substantially reduced if the type of product was known.[9] One feature of special interest is that, apart from Peru which had a single plant producing intermediates, Mexico was the only country where the majority of plants producing *intermediate* products obtained their technology from *nonproducers*. Where the source was known, 65 percent of these plants obtained their technology from process developers or engineering firms, as compared with 45 percent of the full sample. Mexico was also the only country (again apart from the very small Peruvian case of a single plant in this category) in which some plants producing *final* products obtained their technology from *nonproducers*. These atypical findings may reflect the fact that Mexican legislation limiting foreign equity participation is older and stricter than that of the other countries in the sample, reducing somewhat the role of producers, who are usually interested in taking an equity share in recipient entities.

MATURITY OF THE PRODUCT AND PROCESS, AND AGE OF PLANT. In industries conforming to the product life cycle theory, products become standardized as they mature. Initially, transfers are limited, and are undertaken by innovators and later by imitating producers. Over time, however, as the product matures and becomes standardized, nonproducers play an increasing part in transfers. In this subsection we use data on various indicators of maturity to test whether petrochemical technology transfers to Latin America conform to that pattern.

Table 2-3 provides the data on product maturity. It shows the division of transfers of technology between producers and nonproducers, for basic, intermediate, and final products which were first commercialized before 1930, between 1930 and 1940, and after 1940. These time periods were chosen because the 1930–40 period was one of extremely rapid product innovation. During this decade the number of new products equalled that developed over the previous forty years, and was twice the number developed in the years since.

Taking all products together, producers transfer a larger proportion of newer products (accounting for 74 percent of transfers of post-1940 technologies, 70 percent of transfers of technologies developed between

Table 2-2. *Relationship between Type of Licensor and Product Group, by Recipient Country: 280 Petrochemical Plants*

Argentina

Type of licensor	Basic Number	Basic Per-cent	Inter-mediate Number	Inter-mediate Per-cent	Final Number	Final Per-cent	Total Number	Total Per-cent
Producers	3	25	13	68	12	100	28	65
Nonproducers	9	75	6	32	0	0	15	35
All known	12	100	19	100	12	100	43	100
Unknown	2		3		3		8	
Total	14		22		15		51	

Brazil

Type of licensor	Basic Number	Basic Per-cent	Inter-mediate Number	Inter-mediate Per-cent	Final Number	Final Per-cent	Total Number	Total Per-cent
Producers	5	25	16	57	22	100	43	61
Nonproducers	15	75	12	43	0	0	27	39
All known	20	100	28	100	22	100	70	100
Unknown	3		5		2		10	
Total	23		33		24		80	

Chile

Type of licensor	Basic Number	Basic Per-cent	Inter-mediate Number	Inter-mediate Per-cent	Final Number	Final Per-cent	Total Number	Total Per-cent
Producers	0	0	3	75	3	100	6	67
Nonproducers	2	100	1	25	0	0	3	33
All known	2	100	4	100	3	100	9	100
Unknown	2		1		1		4	
Total	4		5		4		13	

Colombia

Type of licensor	Basic Number	Basic Per-cent	Inter-mediate Number	Inter-mediate Per-cent	Final Number	Final Per-cent	Total Number	Total Per-cent
Producers	1	17	6	67	8	100	15	65
Nonproducers	5	83	3	33	0	0	8	35
All known	6	100	9	100	8	100	23	100
Unknown	1		4		0		5	
Total	7		13		8		28	

Mexico

	Basic		Inter-mediate		Final		Total	
	Num-ber	Per-cent	Num-ber	Per-cent	Num-ber	Per-cent	Num-ber	Per-cent
Producers	1	6	8	35	12	86	21	39
Nonproducers	16	94	15	65	2	14	33	61
All known	17	100	23	100	14	100	54	100
Unknown	1		8		5		14	
Total	18		31		19		68	

Peru

	Basic		Inter-mediate		Final		Total	
	Num-ber	Per-cent	Num-ber	Per-cent	Num-ber	Per-cent	Num-ber	Per-cent
Producers	1	33	0	0	1	50	2	33
Nonproducers	2	67	1	100	1	50	4	67
All known	3	100	1	100	2	100	6	100
Unknown	2		6		5		13	
Total	5		7		7		19	

Venezuela

	Basic		Inter-mediate		Final		Total	
	Num-ber	Per-cent	Num-ber	Per-cent	Num-ber	Per-cent	Num-ber	Per-cent
Producers	1	20	5	63	4	100	10	59
Nonproducers	4	80	3	38	0	0	7	41
All known	5	100	8	100	4	100	17	100
Unknown	1		1		2		4	
Total	6		9		6		21	

Full seven-country sample

	Basic		Inter-mediate		Final		Total	
	Num-ber	Per-cent	Num-ber	Per-cent	Num-ber	Per-cent	Num-ber	Per-cent
Producers	12	18	51	55	62	95	125	56
Nonproducers	53	82	41	45	3	5	97	44
All known	65	100	92	100	65	100	222	100
Unknown	12		28		18		58	
Total	77		120		83		280	

Note: All percentages are calculated as proportions of "All known" column subtotals; items may not add to totals because of rounding.

33

Table 2-3. *Relationship between Type of Licensor and Maturity of Product, by Type of Product: 280 Petrochemical Plants*

Type of product and licensor	Pre-1930		1930–40		Post-1940		All known		Total number
	Number	Percent	Number	Percent	Number	Percent	Number	Percent	
Basic products									
Producers	9	18	3	19	0	0	12	18	12
Nonproducers	40	82	13	81	0	0	53	82	53
All known	49	100	16	100	0	0	65	100	
Unknown	10		2		0				12
Total	59		18		0				77
Intermediate products									
Producers	32	55	12	55	7	58	51	55	51
Nonproducers	26	45	10	45	5	42	41	45	41
All known	58	100	22	100	12	100	92	100	
Unknown	17		9		2				28
Total	75		31		14				120

Final products

Producers	10	100	45	94	7	100	62	95	62
Nonproducers	0	0	3	6	0	0	3	5	3
All known	10	100	48	100	7	100	65	100	
Unknown	3		8		7				18
Total	13		56		14				83

All products

Producers	51	44	60	70	14	74	125	56	125
Nonproducers	66	56	26	30	5	26	97	44	97
All known	117	100	86	100	19	100	222	100	
Unknown	30		19		9				58
Total	147		105		28				280

Note: The maturity of a product is determined by the period of its first commercialization in the world. All percentages are calculated as proportions of "All known" column subtotals; items may not add to totals because of rounding.

Table 2-4. Relationship between Type of Licensor and Time Lag between First Application of Process Worldwide and Its First Use in Latin America, by Type of Product: 280 Petrochemical Plants

Type of product and licensor	20+ years Number	20+ years Per cent	15–19 years Number	15–19 years Per cent	10–14 years Number	10–14 years Per cent	5–9 years Number	5–9 years Per cent	Under 5 years Number	Under 5 years Per cent	All known Number	All known Per cent	Un-known number	Total number
Basic products														
Producers	5	42	0	0	1	6	0	0	1	25	7	14	5	12
Nonproducers	7	58	4	100	15	94	13	100	3	75	42	86	11	53
All known	12	100	4	100	16	100	13	100	4	100	49	100		
Unknown	0		0		0		0		0				12	12
Total	12		4		16		13		4				28	77
Intermediate products														
Producers	4	80	6	43	7	44	8	53	4	31	29	46	22	51
Nonproducers	1	20	8	57	9	56	7	47	9	69	34	54	7	41
All known	5	100	14	100	16	100	15	100	13	100	63	100		
Unknown	0		0		0		0		0				28	28
Total	5		14		16		15		13				57	120
Final products														
Producers	4	67	4	100	1	100	11	100	3	100	23	92	39	62
Nonproducers	2	33	0	0	0	0	0	0	0	0	2	8	1	3
All known	6	100	4	100	1	100	11	100	3	100	25	100		
Unknown	0		0		0		0		0				18	18
Total	6		4		1		11		3				58	83
All products														
Producers	13	57	10	45	9	27	19	49	8	40	59	43	66	125
Nonproducers	10	43	12	55	24	73	20	51	12	60	78	57	19	97
All known	23	100	22	100	33	100	39	100	20	100	137	100		
Unknown	0		0		0		0		0				58	58
Total	23		22		33		39		20				143	280

Note: All percentages are calculated as proportions of "All known" column subtotals; items may not add to totals because of rounding.

1930 and 1940, and 44 percent of transfers of pre-1930 ones); nonproducers predominate in transfers of the most mature subgroup, that is, products developed before 1930. If, however, one examines the percentages for basic, intermediate, and final products, it immediately becomes apparent that the relative position of each supplier group varies by product type, but within each product type there is virtually no variation according to the time period in which products were first commercialized in the world. For basic products, the producer/nonproducer split was about 4:1 in favor of nonproducers regardless of product maturity; for intermediates, about 5.5:4.5 in favor of producers; and for final products, nearly 100 percent in favor of producers. Thus the variations for all products reflect the two licensor groups' specialization by type of product—in other words, nonproducers license more basic products (which are relatively old), and producers more final ones (which are relatively new); within each product type, however, the ratios between the two licensor groups show almost no change by maturity period.

A variant on the maturity of the product as an indicator might be the maturity of the process used to make it. (As has already been noted, process innovation can continue even in the case of fully mature and standardized products.) Table 2-4 shows, for the three product types, the share of the two supplier groups in transfers of technology, broken down by the time lag between the processes' first application in the world and their first use in Latin America. The table shows that producers were the source of *all* processes for final products introduced into Latin America with a lag of nineteen years or less after their first application in the world, and that nonproducers dominated the importation of basic processes in a similar way, though to a somewhat lesser degree. In other words, the decisive factor again seems to be the type of product rather than its maturity. In the case of intermediates, with only one exception, producers' role in transfers fell steadily from an 80 percent share of transfers of processes first used in Latin America more than twenty years after initial application worldwide to a share of just over 40 percent for the lags of fifteen to nineteen and ten to fourteen years, and to just over 30 percent for processes first used in Latin America after a lag of only five years.

The maturity of the process can also be defined simply in terms of the year in which it was first used in the world, without reference to the lag between first worldwide application and first use in Latin America. Table 2-5 gives the data, breaking down the processes by the time periods in which they were first used worldwide. The evidence again confirms (in the cases of basic and final products) the two supplier groups' specialization by type of product, and for intermediates and all products it illus-

Table 2-5. *Relationship between Type of Licensor and Period of First Use of Process in the World, by Type of Product: 280 Petrochemical Plants*

Type of product and licensor	Pre-1940		1940–49		1950–54		1955–59	
	Number	Percent	Number	Percent	Number	Percent	Number	Percent
Basic products								
Producers	4	80	1	13	0	0	0	0
Nonproducers	1	20	7	88	3	100	8	100
All known	5	100	8	100	3	100	8	100
Unknown	0		0		0		0	
Total	5		8		3		8	
Intermediate products								
Producers	0	0	7	100	4	57	7	47
Nonproducers	0	0	0	0	3	43	8	53
All known	0	0	7	100	7	100	15	100
Unknown	0		1		1		0	
Total	0		8		8		15	
Final products								
Producers	1	33	6	100	3	100	6	100
Nonproducers	2	67	0	0	0	0	0	0
All known	3	100	6	100	3	100	6	100
Unknown	0		0		0		1	
Total	3		6		3		7	
All products								
Producers	5	63	14	67	7	54	13	45
Nonproducers	3	38	7	33	6	46	16	55
All known	8	100	21	100	13	100	29	100
Unknown	0		1		1		1	
Total	8		22		14		30	

Type of product and licensor	1960–64		Post-1964		All known		Un-known number	Total number
	Number	Percent	Number	Percent	Number	Percent		
Basic products								
Producers	0	0	2	13	7	14	5	12
Nonproducers	9	100	14	88	42	86	11	53
All known	9	100	16	100	49	100		
Unknown	1		0				11	12
Total	10		16				27	77
Intermediate products								
Producers	8	31	6	50	32	48	19	51
Nonproducers	18	69	6	50	35	52	6	41
All known	26	100	12	100	67	100		
Unknown	0		0				26	28
Total	26		12				51	120
Final products								
Producers	8	100	4	100	28	93	34	62
Nonproducers	0	0	0	0	2	7	1	3
All known	8	100	4	100	30	100		
Unknown	1		1				15	18
Total	9		5				50	83
All products								
Producers	16	37	12	38	67	46	58	125
Nonproducers	27	63	20	63	79	54	18	97
All known	43	100	32	100	146	100		
Unknown	2		1				52	58
Total	45		33				128	280

Note: All percentages are calculated as proportions of "All known" column subtotals; items may not add to totals because of rounding.

Table 2-6. *Relationship between Type of Licensor and Period of Plant Construction, by Type of Product: 280 Petrochemical Plants*

Type of product and licensor	Pre-1960		1960-69		Post-1969		All known		Unknown number	Total number
	Number	Percent	Number	Percent	Number	Percent	Number	Percent		
Basic products										
Producers	1	25	8	28	3	9	12	18	0	12
Nonproducers	3	75	21	72	29	91	53	82	0	53
All known	4	100	29	100	32	100	65	100		
Unknown	2		2		6				2	12
Total	6		31		38				2	77
Intermediate products										
Producers	6	100	18	51	21	48	45	54	6	51
Nonproducers	0	0	17	49	23	52	40	46	1	41
All known	6	100	35	100	44	100	85	100		
Unknown	2		6		16				4	28
Total	8		41		60				11	120
Final products										
Producers	7	100	24	92	23	96	54	95	8	62
Nonproducers	0	0	2	8	1	4	3	5	0	3
All known	7	100	26	100	24	100	57	100		
Unknown	2		1		10				5	18
Total	9		27		34				13	83
All products										
Producers	14	82	50	56	47	47	111	54	14	125
Nonproducers	3	18	40	44	53	53	96	46	1	97
All known	17	100	90	100	100	100	207	100		
Unknown	6		9		32				11	58
Total	23		99		132				26	280

Note: All percentages are calculated as proportions of "All known" column subtotals; items may not add to totals because of rounding.

trates the generally declining role of producers in transferring relatively new processes.

The increasing part played in transfers of petrochemical technology by nonproducers (autonomous process developers and engineering firms) during recent years can be demonstrated by data which link producer and nonproducer technology suppliers with the periods when particular plants were built. Table 2-6 shows the information. Ignoring the unknowns as before and taking the totals for all products, nonproducers provided the technologies for 18 percent of plants built before 1960. During the 1960s, their share rose by nearly 250 percent to 44 percent of all plants built. In the years since 1970, the nonproducer group supplied technologies for a majority of all plants built—53 percent. The increasing prominence of nonproducers is also apparent in the subtotals for basic and intermediate products. Again, however, the subtotals by product type show producers supplying the technology for virtually all plants making final products, regardless of when they were built.

Survey data collected (but not reproduced in detail here) on supplier groups' relative participation in transfers according to the stage of the project (whether operational, under construction, being engineered, or still in the planning stage) confirm the trends noted above. In the case of basic products, the producers' share of transfers was 28 percent for completed plants, 11 percent for those being engineered, and zero for those in the planning stage. In the case of intermediates, the producers' share was also highest for completed plants, while the nonproducers' share was highest (reaching 50 percent of the total) for plants not yet constructed. In the case of final products, however, producers continued to dominate the transfer process, even among plants at relatively early stages of development.

SUMMARY AND CONCLUSION. The empirical evidence shows that the type of product rather than its maturity determines whether petrochemical technology is transferred to Latin America by producers or nonproducers. Specific findings from the data presented in this subsection include the following:

• In the case of basic and final products, the pattern of technology transfer is similar to the pattern of ownership. The two supplier groups— chemical and oil firms (producers) on the one hand and process developers and engineering firms (nonproducers) on the other—are even more specialized in their shares of transfers of technologies for these product groups than in their shares of ownership of these technologies. Producers have a virtual monopoly in final products, and nonproducers increasingly predominate in basic products.

• Intermediate products present a less clear picture. If the total number of plants for which each group was the source of technology is taken as a criterion, producers predominate. If, however, one looks at the movement over time in the two groups' shares of transfers, it becomes clear that nonproducers are assuming increasing importance—to the extent of being the transfer agents in over 50 percent of transactions in this subsector in the most recent period.

• Statistical analyses of country-by-country data not reproduced here suggest that recipient country conditions also appear to play some part in determining whether technology is imported from producers or nonproducers. In particular, in countries that impose legal constraints on direct foreign investment (for example, Mexico's law reserving basic and some intermediate petrochemical projects to the government), nonproducers may have an above-average share in transfers, a hypothesis supported in the Mexican case by the summary data in table 2-2. This and other recipient country factors will be discussed further in chapters 3 and 4.

Why are we interested in whether technology is transferred by one type of owner or another? It was suggested in chapter 1 that producers and nonproducers might have different interests and concerns with regard to the transfer process. In particular, it was argued that producers would be likely to want an ownership position in the recipient entity or to include other provisions in the transfer agreement giving them influence over the recipient's post-start-up operations, while nonproducers would not. If this is so, contractual arrangements for transfers can be expected to vary systematically with the type of supplier and, in the light of the evidence presented here, with the type of product. The nature and extent of the two supplier groups' ownership of or influence over recipients, as specified in the transfer agreements they prefer, may in turn have important consequences for recipients' opportunities for learning by doing and indigenous technological development. What are these preferences? The contractual arrangements used by the two groups of core process owners, together with some of their consequences, are discussed in more detail in the next section.

Suppliers' Preferred Contractual Arrangements

Although producers and nonproducers have different approaches to technology transfers, both groups will usually participate to a significant degree in activities associated with a new project. An engineering firm is likely to wish to package the technology, that is, to provide a comprehensive package of *pre-start-up* elements of technical knowledge which includes peripheral technology as well as the relevant core process. An oil or chemical company will be more likely to wish to package the project; it, too, may want to have a say in the provision of pre-start-up services, but it will be especially interested in influencing *post-start-up* questions such as the entity's production level, sources of inputs, exporting plans, and even key operational personnel.

Types of Arrangement Used

Different types of contractual agreement offer licensors different degrees of influence over technology recipients. As will be shown later in this chapter, licensors may exert a substantial degree of influence over a recipient's post-start-up activities even when their ownership position is apparently weak.

The matrix in table 2-7 summarizes in hypothetical terms the main contractual options and their likely consequences. This matrix does not purport to be a comprehensive reflection of the wide variety of arrangements which could be used in practice. It is highly simplified and covers only central tendencies with regard to each type of contractual arrangements. Multiple variations can and do exist, of which only a few examples are listed below:

• With either a straight license agreement or any of the four forms of ownership arrangements, the process owner could exert (or allow an agent selected by him to exert) *total* control over the pre-start-up phase, if

Table 2-7. *Contractual Arrangements and Their Likely Consequences*

		Likely degree of influence over recipient[a]	
Contractual arrangement	*Likely licensor*	*Pre-start-up (transfer)*	*Post-start-up (project operations)*
Straight license	Producer or nonproducer	0 to T	0
Minority licensor participation	Producer	0 to M	m to M
Shared participation	Producer	m to M	M
Majority licensor participation	Producer	M to T	M to T
Subsidiary	Producer	M to T	T

a. 0 = zero influence; m = minor influence; M = major influence; T = total control.

he were to license the technology through a turnkey arrangement under which pre-start-up work was carried out by the process owner himself or a general contractor controlled by him. Such an arrangement might, incidentally, be seen as advantageous by a recipient, or even by a host country government, on the grounds that it would ensure that all the skills necessary for project realization were available and effectively coordinated, that the project would be completed on time and according to the specifications required for implementation of the core technology, and that the process owner or his agent would be taking total responsibility for successful start-up.

• In a highly protected, profitable market where the government either controls a portion of the petrochemical industry itself or has regulations limiting foreign ownership, producers might be willing to provide their technology on a straight license basis.

• In one or two cases, nonproducers have taken ownership positions in recipient entities.[10]

• When a process is transferred for a product which has close substitutes, the bargaining strength of the process owner may be limited; consequently, the potential for obtaining a significant ownership or control position is weak. Under these circumstances, even a producer may be able to exert little or no influence over the recipient's post-start-up activities.

• If the technology owners are producers that have formal or informal links with engineering companies, equipment suppliers, or financing agencies, they are more likely to be interested in a package which includes some degree of influence over pre-start-up as well as post-start-up activities. Similarly, technology suppliers who are nonproducers but have links with sources of equipment and/or financing may wish to incorporate procurement and financing services in their package of pre-start-up services—and the inclusion of these services may limit the recipient's post-start-up freedom of action.

• In some cases, producers will allow a wholly owned subsidiary a substantial degree of effective operational independence, despite their apparent total control.

As noted above, technology suppliers will usually favor transfer arrangements that take the form of packaging the technology or packaging the project. Nonproducer technology owners will be involved in the first type of transfer, but almost never in the second; producers may be involved in both types, but will be particularly concerned with the second.

Packaging the Technology

Technology can be said to be transferred in package form when a single agent other than the recipient supplies or organizes the supply of several or all of the elements of technical knowledge, other than core technology, required to realize a project (these items were defined in chapter 1). The incidence of packaged transfers of petrochemical technology to Latin America reflects both the nature of the technology itself and the characteristics of participants on the supply and demand sides of the transfer process.

Because petrochemical plants have become both larger and more complex in recent years, the transfer of core technology alone may leave the recipients—those on the demand side of the transfer process—with a daunting task of project realization. As will be shown in detail in chapter 3, local technological capability in Latin America is mainly limited to the relatively simple elements of project realization; local capacity to undertake detailed engineering—and, a fortiori, basic engineering—is very limited in most countries.

Thus, despite government regulations designed to inhibit packaging, recipients will often in practice welcome relatively highly packaged transfers. The local unavailability or inferiority (perceived or real) of the skills necessary to transform core technology into a working project means that recipients will often seek a transfer package which includes some or all of the elements of peripheral technology as well.

Meanwhile, on the supply side of the transfer process, the incidence of packaging reflects the evolution of large, multidisciplinary international firms capable of providing recipients with an array of skills broad enough to cover most or all of the technological knowledge needed to realize a project. Both producer and nonproducer firms may supply technology packages, with producers offering arrangements for a packaged project that include supplier participation in post-start-up project operations, and nonproducers packaging the technology into an integrated set of pre-start-up engineering and contracting services. In the case of nonproducers, two situations can be distinguished: when the same firm is both the licensor of the core technology and the supplier of some or all of the peripheral technology needed before start-up; and when one firm is the licensor but another (nonproducer) supplier provides all or most of the technical and organizational services.

The most highly packaged arrangement for transferring technology—and the most complete form of the first type above—is the turnkey contract. Under a contractual arrangement of this kind, a single agent undertakes or supervises the provision of all services required to realize a project. Turnkey contracts can have significant advantages for recipients, such as speed and efficiency of pre-start-up work and, especially, effective coordination of the diverse and complex elements of project planning and implementation. On the supply side, nonproducers are interested in selling as many services as possible and therefore favor a turnkey contract or a similar arrangement, while producers licensing a process are concerned that it will work efficiently after project start-up and therefore favor contractual arrangements that ensure pre-start-up work of the best possible quality. They may also have formal or informal links with particular engineering firms which are familiar with the process concerned and have a proven ability to undertake the engineering and contracting work associated with it. Finally, financing agencies may also favor a turnkey contract as a guarantee of the sound and efficient use of their funds.

Data on the incidence of contractual arrangements involving technology packaging for the 280 plants in our sample are presented in table 2-8. For analytical purposes, four types of transfer arrangements were distinguished:

- The licensor (L) also undertook the engineering (E) and contracting (C) functions, the latter being defined as the services required to build and equip the plant. This type of transfer is represented in the table by $L = E = C$.
- The licensor also undertook the engineering function, but a third party was responsible for contracting work $(L = E \neq C)$.
- A single firm undertook both engineering and contracting work, but was not the licensor $(L \neq E = C)$.
- The three functions were separate $(L \neq E \neq C)$.

The first arrangement is clearly the most highly packaged and approximates a turnkey contract. Overall, these most highly packaged contractual arrangements represented nearly half (81 out of 167, or 48.5 percent) of the cases where the type of arrangement was known. The least packaged type of arrangement was found in only six cases (3.6 percent). Cases in which the engineering and contracting functions were carried out by local firms in the recipient country were rare: data collected in our 280-plant sample showed that in only 12 cases out of 180 was engineering in the hands of local firms, and in only 28 out of 160 were contracting services supplied locally.

Table 2-8 also shows the distribution of the incidence of the four types of contractual arrangement according to a number of key variables. Some of the main findings that can be drawn from the table are:

• Transfers of technology for plants producing basic and intermediate products were much more likely to be highly packaged than those involving final products.

• The incidence of highly packaged transfers was greater for more recently constructed plants than for older ones. This probably reflects the increasing scale and complexity of petrochemical operations and the trend for nonproducers—who prefer this type of contract—to account for an increasing share of transfers.

• Nonproducers were more likely to be involved in highly packaged transfers than producers, and they accounted for 51 of the 81 turnkey type of transfers, or 63 percent. This is what one would expect: nonproducers specialize in basic and intermediate products, where problems of plant scale are more important and the provision of pre-start-up services is at the heart of their business. In a sense, the surprising fact about this particular data set is how high the incidence of the turnkey type of arrangement is for the producer group.

• Straight license agreements accounted for 58 out of 81 (72 percent) of the turnkey type of transfer, and highly packaged transfers of this kind made up half of all the straight license agreements whose contractual terms were known. Thus, agreements of this kind may not restrict recipients' post-start-up activities, but nevertheless frequently involve extensive supplier participation in pre-start-up work.

• Of the seven countries, Brazil was by far the most frequent user of the most highly packaged type of arrangement, and Mexico was equally prominent in the category in which the licensor also undertakes project engineering.

• With regard to maturity factors, the incidence of highly packaged transfers was most frequent for the most mature products for which technology was transferred. No clear trend emerged in terms of maturity of process: packaging of all three types appeared to peak for processes first used between 1955 and 1964, however.

In general, the data clearly show that the incidence of some form of technology packaging is high and rising; that it is mainly (but by no means wholly) associated with transfers in which the licensor is a nonproducer and the product to be manufactured is in the basic or intermediate category; and that the most highly packaged form of transfer is the one most frequently used.

Despite the negative effects of packaging in terms of externalities and social costs, the benefits of technology packaging may, of course, gen-

Table 2-8. Technology Packaging, by Selected Indicators: 280 Petrochemical Plants

Indicator	L = E = C Number	L = E = C Percent	L = E ≠ C Number	L = E ≠ C Percent	L ≠ E = C Number	L ≠ E = C Percent	L ≠ E ≠ C Number	L ≠ E ≠ C Percent	All known number	Un-known number	Total number
Type of product											
Basic	34	58	11	19	12	20	2	4	59	18	77
Intermediate	38	52	18	25	15	20	2	3	73	47	120
Final	9	26	10	29	14	40	2	6	35	48	83
Total	81	49	39	23	41	25	6	4	167	113	280
Period of plant construction											
Before 1960	4	57	2	29	1	14	0	0	7	16	23
1960–69	33	46	12	17	21	30	5	7	71	28	99
1970 and after	43	50	23	27	19	22	1	1	86	46	132
Unknown	1	33	2	67	0	0	0	0	3	23	26
Total	81	49	39	23	41	25	6	4	167	113	280
Type of supplier											
Producer	30	38	14	18	29	37	5	6	78	47	125
Nonproducer	51	57	25	28	12	13	1	1	89	8	97
Unknown	0	0	0	0	0	0	0	0	0	58	58
Total	81	49	39	23	41	25	6	4	167	113	280
Type of contractual agreement											
Straight license	58	50	29	25	25	21	4	3	116	32	148
Minority participation	16	53	4	13	8	27	2	7	30	7	37
Shared participation	0	0	1	100	0	0	0	0	1	1	2
Majority participation	0	0	2	67	1	33	0	0	3	9	12
Subsidiary	6	40	3	20	6	40	0	0	15	15	30
Local technology	1	100	0	0	0	0	0	0	1	2	3
Unknown	0	0	0	0	1	100	0	0	1	47	48
Total	81	49	39	23	41	25	6	4	167	113	280

	L = E = C		L = E ≠ C		L ≠ E = C		L ≠ E ≠ C		All known	Unknown	Total
	No.	%	No.	%	No.	%	No.	%			
Recipient country											
Argentina	9	32	7	25	11	39	1	4	28	23	51
Brazil	30	56	9	17	12	22	3	6	54	26	80
Colombia	12	67	3	17	3	17	0	0	18	10	28
Chile	4	80	1	20	0	0	0	0	5	8	13
Mexico	10	25	17	42	11	27	2	5	40	28	68
Peru	5	83	0	0	1	17	0	0	6	13	19
Venezuela	11	69	2	12	3	19	0	0	16	5	21
Total	81	49	39	23	41	25	6	4	167	113	280
First commercialization of product											
Before 1930	59	63	19	20	14	15	2	2	94	53	147
1930–40	15	26	17	29	22	38	4	7	58	47	105
After 1940	7	47	3	20	5	33	0	0	15	13	28
Total	81	49	39	23	41	25	6	4	167	113	280
First use of technology											
Before 1955	12	39	7	23	10	32	2	6	31	13	44
1955–64	33	53	13	21	14	23	2	3	62	13	75
1965 and after	13	46	8	28	6	21	1	4	28	5	33
Unknown	23	50	11	24	11	24	1	2	46	82	128
Total	81	49	39	23	41	25	6	4	167	113	280

Key: L = E = C   Licensor is also responsible for engineering and contracting (turnkey contract).
L = E ≠ C   Licensor is also responsible for engineering but not for contracting.
L ≠ E = C   Engineering and contracting are in the hands of the same entity, but licensor is a separate entity.
L ≠ E ≠ C   Licensor and entities responsible for engineering and contracting are all separate parties.

Note: All percentages are calculated as proportions of "All known" row subtotals; items may not add to 100 percent because of rounding.

uinely outweigh their social as well as private costs. The opportunity costs to the host country's economy of building up local sources of the knowledge required need to be taken into consideration; for example, both Japan and the Republic of Korea initially imported technology in a highly packaged form, although they rapidly began to unpackage it. Nevertheless, the loss of opportunities for technological development through learning by doing, by the recipient entity as well as by local engineering contractors, also need to be borne in mind. This question will be discussed further in chapter 3.

Packaging the Project

Technology owners who are also producers often participate in transfers of relatively highly packaged pre-start-up services. Unlike nonproducers, however, they will also tend to be interested in contractual arrangements that give them some say in the recipients' post-start-up operations. The straightforward reason is that the recipients will be entering the same product market as the technology owners themselves. In particular, producers who license their technology will wish to maximize their return on transfer transactions and to ensure that the recipient's output meshes with (or at least does not conflict with) their own worldwide or regional production and marketing strategies. This subsection examines in some detail the various types of arrangements preferred by this group of technology suppliers.

Whether a producer who supplies a technology to a new entity will set up a wholly owned subsidiary, take a majority shareholding in the new entity, accept an equal or minority equity share, or license the technology in exchange for royalties depends on a number of factors. Some international producer companies concentrate their activities on a particular group of clients or a particular group of products (fertilizers, for example), while others base their competitive strength on the sale of a diversified range of products to a large number of different markets. Firms of the first type tend to prefer to set up a wholly owned subsidiary or to take a majority holding in a recipient entity, so as to take advantage of organizational economies of scale and to promote effective centralized decisionmaking. Companies of the second type will be likely to prefer less comprehensive involvement and to encourage a degree of local autonomy in decisionmaking, especially where local market conditions are uncertain. In these circumstances the supplier may well be content with a minority shareholding.

A relatively low level of equity participation on the part of the technology supplier has the advantage of reducing his financial and political risks. There may be other advantages if the recipient entity is already established and has a strong local market position—especially since even minority participation can give the technology supplier leverage, sometimes of a decisive kind.

In other cases the technology supplier may settle for a licensing arrangement without any ownership position in the recipient entity. This type of arrangement is likely to be used when the sector or subsector concerned is owned by the government (basic petrochemicals in Mexico, for example) or where the perceived risks of investing are very high. Licensing may also be the preferred option if the supplier is a relatively small company which cannot afford heavy direct investment or operational involvement in overseas ventures, or where the product to be manufactured faces strong competition from close substitutes and the supplier is consequently in a poor bargaining position. Even when transfers take place through licensing arrangements, suppliers may still be able to influence recipients' operational decisions through conditions in the license agreements.

Table 2-9 provides summary survey data on the types of contractual arrangements used for 127 transfers completed or being undertaken by suppliers who are also producers. The different arrangements used are broken down by the stage of the project; that is, whether it is already constructed, under construction, being engineered, or still in the planning stage. In the case of the 97 existing plants, although a surprisingly high proportion of transfers was undertaken through license agreements (22 of the 94 cases in which the type of arrangement is known, or 23 percent), wholly owned subsidiaries are the most frequently used type of arrangement (26 cases, or 28 percent of those where the arrangement is known), followed by minority participation (24 percent) and majority participation (21 percent). Fifty-fifty ownership arrangements are very infrequent (3 percent).

The situation changes in an interesting way when plants still in the construction, engineering, or planning stages are examined. Of the 28 transfer agreements for plants not yet in operation at the time the survey was undertaken, 17 (63 percent of the 27 where the type of agreement was known) involved minority participation, and another six (22 percent) involved straight licensing arrangements. Wholly owned subsidiaries and majority participations were much less frequent (with two agreements, or only 7 percent of total known agreements, in each case). The data thus suggest a shift in the pattern of contractual arrangements for newer plants in favor of less heavy investment in recipient entities. Although the proportion of straight license agreements for projected plants actually fell slightly, that of minority participation rose sharply and that of sub-

Table 2-9. Type of Contractual Agreement, by Project Stage, When Technology Is Supplied by Producer Firms: 127 Petrochemical Plants

Type of agreement	Constructed		Under construction		Engineering		Planning		Stage unknown (number)	Total number
	Number	Percent	Number	Percent	Number	Percent	Number	Percent		
Straight license	22	23	2	40	2	14	2	25	0	28
Minority participation	23	24	1	20	11	79	5	63	0	40
Shared participation	3	3	0	0	0	0	0	0	0	3
Majority participation	20	21	0	0	1	7	1	13	1	23
Subsidiary	26	28	2	40	0	0	0	0	1	29
All known	94	100	5	100	14	100	8	100	2	123
Participation, but extent unknown	3		0		0		0		0	3
Unknown whether any participation	0		1		0		0		0	1
Total	97		6		14		8		2	127

Note: All percentages are calculated as proportions of "All known" column subtotals; items may not add to totals because of rounding.

sidiaries and majority participation fell sharply compared with agreements for existing plants.

ARRANGEMENTS TO SECURE SUPPLIERS' EARNINGS FROM TRANSFERS. Table 2-10 shows the distribution by individual producer firms of the 127 contractual agreements covered by table 2-9. Of interest here is the extent to which the same producer is willing to enter into different types of agreement—sometimes as radically different as straight license and wholly owned subsidiary. This apparent flexibility suggests that the producers shown in the table—most of whom are chemical companies—may be willing to adjust contractual arrangements to local market conditions or government policies (see chapter 3). Nevertheless, arrangements can be made whereby a producer shares in the income flows resulting from a transfer or secures operational influence over post-start-up activities, even when the producer's overt participation in the recipient's equity is relatively small.

The direct or explicit earnings accruing to producers who transfer technology can take the following main forms:

- Dividends, which will be related to the recipient's total profits and the supplier's participation in those profits through his equity holding
- Royalties, which will be related to the recipient's actual or estimated total sales or output and to the royalty payment arrangements specified in the transfer agreement. Royalties may be expressed in terms of a monetary amount per unit of output or in terms of a flat percentage of the value of sales.
- A straight lump-sum payment for the technology transferred
- Service payments for technical assistance of various kinds.

Table 2-11 illustrates the kinds of payments which selected suppliers of core technology who are also producers receive under different kinds of arrangements.

A supplier's preference among the first three items in the list above will depend to a large degree on his perception of the risks and uncertainties involved in the venture for which technology has been transferred, and on the effects of taxes, exchange controls, and other regulations on different forms of payment.

With regard to uncertainty, dividends clearly represent the riskiest option for the supplier, since their value depends on the amount that the supplier is prepared to invest in the recipient's equity and the degree of profitability of the recipient's operations. Royalties are a somewhat less risky form of payment, since the supplier does not have to make a net

Table 2-10. *Producers That Supplied Process Technology and Type of Contractual Agreement Used: 127 Petrochemical Plants*
(number of agreements)

| Producer | Country | Participation | | | | | | | | |
		Straight license	Minor- ity	Shared	Major- ity	Extent un- known	Sub- sidiary	Local tech- nology	Un- known	Total
Allied Chemical	United States	1	0	0	0	0	0	0	0	1
Atlantic Richfield	United States	1	0	0	0	0	0	0	0	1
Borden Chemical	United States	1	0	0	2	0	2	0	0	5
Cabot Carbon	United States	0	1	0	0	0	2	0	0	3
Chevron Chemical	United States	1	0	0	0	0	0	0	0	1
Colcar (Columbian Carbon)	United States	1	0	0	1	0	0	0	0	2
Dart Industries	United States	0	1	0	0	0	0	0	0	1
Diamond Shamrock	United States	1	0	1	0	2	0	0	0	4
Dow Chemicals	United States	1	0	1	3	0	3	0	0	8
Firestone Tyre and Rubber	United States	1	0	0	0	0	0	0	0	1
Foster Grant	United States	0	1	0	0	0	0	0	0	1
Goodyear Tire and Rubber	United States	0	1	0	0	0	0	0	0	1
B. F. Goodrich	United States	0	3	0	0	0	1	0	0	4
Halcon	United States	0	1	0	0	1	0	0	0	1
Hercules	United States	1	1	0	0	0	0	0	0	2
Hooker Chemical	United States	0	0	0	0	0	1	0	0	1
Koppers	United States	0	2	0	4	1	0	0	0	7
Monsanto	United States	0	0	0	0	0	5	0	0	5
National Distillers	United States	0	1	0	0	0	0	0	0	1
Phillips Petroleum	United States	2	4	0	0	0	1	0	0	7
Reichhold Chemicals	United States	0	0	0	0	0	1	0	0	1
Spencer Chemicals	United States	1	0	0	0	0	0	0	0	1
Texas & U.S. Rubber	United States	0	1	0	0	0	0	0	0	1

Company	Country									Total
Unicarbon (United Carbon)	United States	0	0	0	0	0	0	1	0	1
Union Carbide	United States	1	0	0	0	0	0	2	0	3
Badische Anilin-und-Soda Fabrik	Germany, Fed. Rep. of	1	0	0	0	0	0	4	0	5
Bayer	Germany, Fed. Rep. of	0	0	0	0	0	0	0	0	1
Hoechst	Germany, Fed. Rep. of	1	1	0	1	0	0	1	0	3
Witten Dynamite Nobel	Germany, Fed. Rep. of	2	1	0	0	0	0	0	0	3
Distillers (British Petroleum)	United Kingdom	3	0	0	0	0	0	0	0	3
Imperial Chemical Industries	United Kingdom	1	4	0	0	0	1	0	0	6
Asahi Chemicals	Japan	1	0	0	0	0	0	0	0	1
Mitsubishi Chemical	Japan	0	2	0	0	0	0	0	0	2
Nippon Zeon	Japan	1	0	0	0	0	0	0	0	1
Sumitomo	Japan	0	1	0	0	0	0	0	0	1
Toyo Koatsu	Japan	2	0	0	0	0	0	0	0	2
Montedison	Italy	7	1	0	0	0	0	0	0	8
Chemie Technip	France	1	0	0	0	0	0	0	0	1
Ethylene Plastique	France	0	1	0	0	0	0	0	0	1
Pechiney Saint Gobain	France	2	1	0	0	0	0	0	0	3
Rhone Poulenc	France	0	1	0	1	0	2	0	0	4
Solvay	Belgium	0	1	0	0	0	2	0	0	3
Union Chemique Belge	Belgium	1	0	0	0	0	0	0	0	1
Shell Development	United Kingdom and Netherlands	1	0	0	0	0	0	0	1	1
Polcorp (Polymer Corp.)	Canada	0	0	0	0	0	0	0	0	2
Perstorp	Sweden	3	1	0	0	0	0	0	0	1
Osterreichische Hiag	Austria	1	0	0	0	0	0	0	0	3
Local producer firms		0	0	0	0	0	3	3	0	3
Total		41	36	2	12	3	29	3	1	127

Table 2-11. *Capitalization of Royalties and Financial Investment in Selected Joint Ventures with Government Participation*

| Case | Type of firm | Per-centage partic-ipation of tech-nology supplier | Lump-sum payment (U.S. dollars) | Form of payment | Other payments | | | Value of foreign partner's shares (U.S. dollars) | Financial investment (U.S. dollars) |
					Technical assistance	Royalties	Other		
1	JVGLF⁻	15	254,000	Three install-ments	$100 a day per person: $24,000	None	0	254,000	None
2	JVGLF⁻	8.18	1,103,450	$459,770 to buy shares; $643,678 in three install-ments	$46 a day per person: $100,000	None	0	2,761,000	1,637,500
3	JVGLF⁻	25	450,000	To buy 25% of shares	$150 a day per person	0.35 cent per pound of product 1; 3% of net sales of product 2	0	450,000	None
4	JVGLF⁻	30	1,722,800	To buy 30% of shares	Salaries and expenses	$737.494; 0.023 cent per kilogram over 50,000 tons a year	0	1,722,800	None

5	JVGF⁻	25	1,200,000	To buy 25% of shares		Quarterly 2% net sales first year; 2.5% net sales second year; 3% net sales thereafter	0	2,045,500	May be extra investment of $845,500 or price of technology may have risen	None
6	JVGLF⁻	33⅓	533,600	Three installments	$18,500	Guaranteed: $318,380	Lump-sum includes engineering	533,600	None
7	JVGLF⁻	10	208,800	To buy 10% of shares		Continuous royalties over 16 years	$100,000 yearly for continuous know-how	208,800	None
8	JVG/F	50	400,000	To buy shares		Royalties on sales	Engineering services, $1,485,000	2,000,000	1,600,000
9	JVGF⁺	70	2,000,000	To buy shares		4.5% of sales of product 1; 3.5% of sales of product 2	Credit parent company, $1,420,000	8,580,000	6,580,000
10	JVGF⁻	15	600,000	To buy 15% of shares		From 3.55% to 5% of net sales yearly		600,000	None

Key: JV = joint venture; G = public enterprises; L = local private firms; F⁻ = foreign minority participation; F⁺ = foreign majority participation.

outlay to obtain his return, and sales or output (the usual basis for such payments) are less likely to be subject to violent fluctuations than are profits. Arrangements for straightforward royalty payments do not in themselves give the supplier any control over the recipient's post-start-up activities, however. A lump-sum payment bears the least risk and is therefore preferred by nonproducer suppliers of technology, who are generally smaller—and therefore less able to accept large risks—than chemical or oil companies and are also more subject to cyclical fluctuations in their business. The drawback to lump-sum payments is that they offer the supplier no inherent potential either for participation in the recipient entity's earnings after start-up or for involvement in its post-start-up operations. As already noted, this question is generally of little concern to nonproducers but may be of great importance to licensors who are also producers.

Tax regimes, exchange controls, and other regulations may lead suppliers to choose different forms of payment for their services. For example, in some suppliers' countries of origin (such as the United States) income in the form of dividends is allowed the privilege of deferral, so that tax is not payable on such income until it is actually repatriated to the country of origin. On the other hand, most host countries permit the deduction of royalties, but not dividends, from taxable income; and most exchange control regimes restrict the repatriation of dividends to overseas suppliers of technology much more sharply than the repatriation of royalties. Suppliers will vary the forms of payment for their services in the light of these and other regulatory considerations and in accordance with the questions of risk outlined in the previous paragraph.

In practice, the contractual arrangement preferred by core technology suppliers who are also producers appears to be a combination of a lump sum representing capitalization of a proportion of expected royalties (which the supplier may then convert into an equity shareholding in the recipient entity without actually having to lay out his own capital) plus regular royalty payments based on the value of sales or the volume of output. From the supplier's point of view, such an arrangement offers a helpful blend of part-ownership and income. Supplier participation (both financial and operational) in post-start-up activities may also appear attractive to the recipients. Their risk would seem to be reduced (because their recurrent expenditures are lowered by the proportion of royalties capitalized), and their opportunities for incorporating the supplier's proven management or marketing expertise into their activities would seem to be enhanced.

Most of the examples in table 2-11 involve various permutations of a package which includes a lump-sum payment plus a flow of royalties; in one case, the agreement specifies a minimum level of royalties. The lump-sum capitalization of royalties is converted to equity in virtually every case; in some cases suppliers have invested additional amounts in the recipient entity, thereby increasing their ownership position.

The fourth item listed earlier was payment for technical assistance provided by the supplier. Technical assistance can take various forms, including management and/or marketing services, quality control, and trouble-shooting and may be perceived by the recipients to be to their advantage. Payments for technical assistance are recorded in six of the ten sample agreements shown in table 2-11.

In addition to direct payments explicitly set out in the transfer agreement, suppliers may have other opportunities for deriving income from recipients. These include transfer pricing on interaffiliate sales and interest payments on interaffiliate loans. The first occurs when the supplier or an affiliate provides the recipient with inputs such as raw material, intermediate products, or capital goods at prices higher than those pertaining on the open market. The relatively high tariffs on intermediate goods in most recipient countries, and the fact that the raw material or undifferentiated intermediates required for most processes have reasonably well-established world market prices, set limits on the opportunities for transfer pricing of inputs in the petrochemical industry. In the case of capital equipment, transfer pricing is more likely in technology transfers undertaken by nonproducing suppliers (for example, engineering firms) which, as noted in chapter 2, may have formal or informal links with firms that manufacture equipment or machinery.

Data collected but not reproduced in detail here suggest that interest payments on interaffiliate loans may be used by some suppliers of petrochemical technology to increase the flow of income from recipients. Survey findings about debt-equity ratios of a sample of seventeen firms in Latin America suggest that the ratio may be higher for those in which foreign corporations have relatively large equity holdings. The evidence is limited, indirect, and inconclusive, however.

In countries which limit the direct remission of profits, suppliers may raise the level of royalty payments to compensate for ceilings on direct remission. For example, in the Colombian rubber industry, domestic firms paid an average of about 10 percent of their profits as royalties, while subsidiaries of foreign companies paid out a much higher proportion—about 53 percent.[11] Thus royalties, generally considered to be a form of direct compensation for the right to use technology acquired, can also be used for the indirect remission of profits derived from the use of the technology by the recipient.

ARRANGEMENTS TO SECURE SUPPLIERS' OPERATIONAL INFLUENCE OVER RECIPIENTS. The remainder of this chapter will briefly sketch some of the methods that suppliers can use to influence the day-to-day or strategic operational decisions of recipient entities. It should perhaps be reemphasized at this point that this study is concerned with the contractual arrangements associated with a particular set of technology transfers. Our purpose here is simply to describe these arrangements, using actual contracts entered into by petrochemical technology suppliers and recipients in Latin America as our data base. The much larger and more problematical task of systematically judging the economic or political consequences of these arrangements—let alone their desirability—is beyond the scope of the data we have collected. Thus, terms such as "influence" or "monopoly" are to be read as descriptions of what is, rather than as quasi-value judgments about what should or should not be.

When suppliers who are themselves producers hold an ownership position in the recipient entity (even a minority shareholding) they can use this stake to exert an influence on recipients' post-start-up operations which may be disproportionately large in relation to their percentage of equity. In particular, suppliers can exert influence through (a) the decisionmaking process laid down in the by-laws of the proposed recipient entity; (b) the choice of local partners in the entity; and (c) marketing arrangements for the sale of the recipients' output through backward integration or exclusive marketing rights.

Decisionmaking processes can be designed to favor a foreign partner, even when he is a minority shareholder. One method is to require that decisions of the board of directors be approved by a minimum number of directors, with the number set in such a way that decisions cannot be approved unless the representatives of the foreign partner on the board agree. Another way is to specify explicitly in the by-laws that the foreign partner's representatives must approve any decision taken. This method was used in five of the eight Venezuelan cases on which we collected detailed data. Alternatively, the percentage of shareholders required to ratify a board decision or to put forward a shareholders' initiative to the board can be fixed so high that foreign equity owners' concurrence must be obtained. Again, five of the eight Venezuelan cases—including all three cases not covered by the second stipulation noted above—needed a 75 percent level of shareholder approval, and in two of these five cases the foreign partner's equity share was 30 percent or more. Provisions of these kinds render nugatory the stipulation, frequently made by the governments of developing countries, that local interests have a 51 percent shareholding in any joint venture—because their 51 percent is insufficient to validate a decision.

The choice of local partners can also help ensure that the interests of suppliers who are themselves producers are not ignored once the technology has been transferred and the new entity has become operational. If locally held equity is either very widely dispersed among a larger number of shareholders or in the hands of a local partner who lacks interest in or knowledge of the entity's day-to-day management, the foreign partner may be able effectively to control operations, even if he has a minority shareholding.

The data collected showed little evidence of wide dispersion of shareholding. In addition, local state-owned petrochemical entities or other government agencies participated in 50 of the 95 joint ventures with foreign partners identified in the data. In such cases management decisions are likely to be aligned relatively closely with local priorities, but the extent of government participation varies sharply from country to country. (This and other factors related to the recipients of petrochemical technology in Latin America will be discussed more extensively in chapter 3.)

The technology supplier can also influence the operations of a licensee through marketing arrangements for the sale of the new plant's products. Such arrangements may include a process of backward integration, whereby a plant is set up to produce intermediates for sale to a previously established plant manufacturing final products.[12] Foreign producers enter a developing country's market by initially establishing subsidiaries to manufacture final products and subsequently create joint ventures with government or local partners to produce the inputs needed for these products. Arrangements of this kind have several advantages for the foreign partner. First, he can enter the production chain at its least risky stage, when plant size—and therefore investment—is relatively small. Second, he can prove to the government that there is an unsatisfied demand for the inputs needed for the final products; he can then suggest that these inputs be manufactured locally to save foreign exchange—and can take advantage of the investment incentives usually provided for this kind of project. Third, he can charge low prices for the products of the firm set up to supply the inputs required (whose profits he shares with a state enterprise or a private local partner) and can thus obtain extra profits on the final products from the plant in which he is the principal shareholder.

In some cases exclusive marketing rights are granted to foreign partners who have not supplied technology but have access to an international marketing system. Examples of this practice are two ventures for the manufacture of intermediate products in Venezuela and one in Argentina. In one joint venture in Venezuela, one foreign partner (who is not the technology supplier) owns 15 percent of the equity and has exclusive rights to the plant's output. In a second joint venture, for the production of ammonia, the foreign partner is a marketing company rather than a producer, owns 49 percent of the firm's equity, and has exclusive distribution rights. In Argentina, another joint venture for the production of ammonia has granted distribution rights to a local firm and a subsidiary of Shell, each of whom holds 18.6 percent of the company's equity.

Even without equity participation, the licensor may include conditions in the license agreement which effectively safeguard his interests. He can, for example, sign a management contract with the recipient, under which ownership of the recipient entity is wholly or mainly in the hands of local interests but the technology supplier (or a management group nominated by him) undertakes operational management in return for a fee. It has been argued that management contracts have important advantages for both supplier and recipient, in that they provide the supplier with the opportunity to oversee day-to-day operations without having to make any direct investment, while the recipient retains ownership of the entity.[13] The management contract might also offer the recipient such advantages as high standards of operational efficiency and opportunities for learning how to operate the plant with his own personnel after the contract expires.

The counterarguments to these propositions contend that ownership per se is of relatively little importance and that one of the key issues in the debate about the relative costs and benefits of technology transfer is in fact the question of day-to-day operational control—precisely what the management contract concept surrenders to the supplier or a developed-country firm nominated by him. Another argument is that management contracts need not in fact guarantee the recipient an efficiently run plant, because the management group may have motives other than maximizing efficiency, and these may affect its decisionmaking.[14] Management contracts can also be used to raise the share of income accruing to the technology supplier even if he has no equity participation.[15] Furthermore, it is argued, management contracts place virtually all risks on the recipient, whereas in fact the supplier is more able to accept risk factors because he is more able to diversify them.

More generally, producers who license their technology may insert self-protective clauses into transfer agreements, which the recipients must accept if they want the transfer to take place, regardless of whether the supplier participates in the recipient's equity. Examination of a sample of technology agreements provides a number of examples of conditions of this kind, some of which are briefly described below.

The technology supplier whose earnings from the transfer are based on lump-sum payments or royalty flows may protect the value of these earnings by clauses in the transfer agreement that guarantee minimum royalties or interest penalties for late payment of scheduled amounts. In addition, payments are almost invariably quoted in the technology supplier's currency to protect against foreign exchange risks.

Licensing agreements frequently stipulate the maximum output of the plant and require the consent of the licensor for any expansion. Clauses of this sort can inhibit the learning-by-doing process by precluding experimentation with specifications and equipment. The learning-by-doing process can also be inhibited by technology agreements of long duration which may prevent the recipients from altering the plant or experimenting with the equipment, and leave them with outdated technology at the end of the agreement. An analysis of eleven technology agreements which formed part of the data base for this study shows that the average length of the agreements was eleven years, with a range from seven to sixteen years. The issue of obsolescence does not arise, of course, if a contract specifies that the technology supplier will keep the recipient up-to-date with regard to any improvements to the process. Moreover, contracts rarely incorporate penalty clauses for breaking the agreement before its termination date.

The duration of the agreement seems to increase as the product approaches the final demand end of the production chain, probably because the technology for basic and many intermediate products tends to be provided by engineering firms which are not interested in long-term post-start-up contracts. In addition, the longer duration of contracts for final products may reflect the value placed by *recipients* on the right to use the products' brand names—which may have a longer effective economic life than the technology they embody—and on the opportunity to obtain information on process improvements from the supplier for as long as possible.[16]

The technology owner can also secure his rights over the licensed technology through grant-back clauses which stipulate that he be informed of any improvements made in the technology by the recipient firm. In petrochemicals this is usually a reciprocal obligation—and, like a long-term contract, may be considered desirable by recipients because it allows the licensee to take advantage of improvements made by the supplier or other recipients.

Clauses regarding confidentiality are found in all technology contracts. They oblige both parties to keep secret all technical information transferred during the lifetime of the contract, a period which may well exceed the useful life of the information transferred. By limiting the diffusion of the transferred technology, this clause can also limit the learning process. The recipient is as likely as the technology owner to consider confidentiality beneficial, however, because it gives the recipient a temporary monopoly in his own country.

Agreements often include clauses to protect the licensor against competition from his own licensees by restricting their exports to third-country markets.[17] For example, a clause in a nonexclusive license to produce an intermediate used in the fabrication of nylon establishes the right of the licensee to sell throughout the world, except in the United States and its territories and the United Kingdom. A similar clause in another nonexclusive license to produce thermoplastics prohibits sales to Japan. In both these cases the technology supplier is a minority partner in the recipient firm (8.8 percent and 30 percent respectively). Limitations on the volume of production may also implicitly restrict exports. Because of the importance of economies of scale in the petrochemical industry, restrictions on plant size and output can effectively prohibit production at prices that are competitive on world markets. The tendency toward overvalued exchange rates in developing countries, however, may be as potent an impediment to exporting as implicit or explicit contractual restrictions.

In the past, licensors tried to safeguard their position by specifying in contracts that any controversy or arbitration was to be settled in the courts of the licensor's country. Recent Latin American legislation on foreign investment and technology transfer has, however, given greater rights to licensees and has virtually ruled out the use of any outside courts, especially those of suppliers' countries, for the arbitration of disputes.

Transfer agreements may also give the technology owner the right to appoint important personnel. In the absence of a specific clause about the selection of personnel, most licensing agreements are signed together with a technical assistance contract which stipulates that the technology owner can send specialized personnel to advise on or supervise detailed engineering, procurement, assembly, start-up, and initial operation of the plant.

Finally, as noted earlier, the licensor may reserve the right to designate the firm responsible for the design and construction of the plant. Basic engineering is frequently carried out by the owner of the process or by an engineering firm that has collaborated in scaling up the process. Local capability for basic engineering is extremely limited in Latin America, but the capacity to undertake detailed engineering is available in a number of countries (Argentina, Brazil, and Mexico, for example; see chapter 3). Under clauses of the kind mentioned above, however, these services must be contracted to engineering firms selected by the process owner, who can also influence the selection of engineering firms and other contractors through his participation on the recipient's board.

Thus, suppliers can incorporate various clauses into the contractual arrangements to safeguard their interests—even when they have little or no share in the recipient entities' equity. As noted earlier, recipients may often perceive it to be in their interest, as well as in that of suppliers, to make relatively highly packaged pre-start-up transfer arrangements (such as turnkey contracts) or post-start-up arrangements under which the supplier has an equity share in the recipient entity or otherwise participates in operations without equity. Under certain conditions, recipients can, if they wish, limit suppliers' participation to a lesser extent than the suppliers might regard as desirable.

Notes

1. John Roberts, "Engineering Consultancy, Industrialization and Development," in Charles Cooper (ed.), *Science, Technology and Development: The Political Economy of Technical Advance in Underdeveloped Countries* (London: Frank Cass, 1973).

2. For example, the Badger Company has collaborated with producers such as Standard Oil of Ohio (Sohio), Union Carbide, the Cosden Oil and Chemical Company, Sherwin Williams, and B. F. Goodrich in the development or scaling up of various processes. Similarly, M. W. Kellogg has collaborated with ICI, and Lummus has collaborated with Monsanto, Union Carbide, and Shell in a number of process development projects. See C. Freeman, "Chemical Process Plant: Innovation and the World Market," *National Institute Economic Review*, no. 45 (August 1968).

3. Examples of this practice are the ICI low-pressure process for the production of methanol, which is licensed through Kellogg, Humphrey and Glasgow, Power Gas, Uhde, and Chemico; and Shell's ethylene glycol process, which is licensed through Fluor, Kellogg, and Lummus.

4. Firms of this type active in Latin America include Lummus, Foster Wheeler, Fluor, Badger, Lurgi, Technip, Techint, Snam Progetti, and M. W. Kellogg.

5. Subsidiaries of process owners include Uhde, a subsidiary of Hoechst; Snam Progetti, a subsidiary of Ente Nazionale de Idrocarburi (ENI); Stamicarbon, a subsidiary of Dutch State Mines; Technip, a subsidiary of Institut Français du Pétrole (IFP); Procon, a subsidiary of Universal Oil Products; Toyo Engineering Company, a subsidiary of Mitsui Toatsu Chemicals; Pechiney Saint Gobain, which is associated with Rhone-Progil; Instituto Mexicano de Petróleo (IMP), a subsidiary of Pemex; and Scientific Design, a subsidiary of Halcon International. Subsidiaries of industrial or financial groups include the Badger Company, a subsidiary of Raytheon; Chemical Construction Corporation, a subsidiary of the Aerojet General Corporation (owned by General Tire and Rubber); M. W. Kellogg, a subsidiary of Pullman; Lummus, a subsidiary of Combustion Engineering; and Inventa, a member of the Ems Group of Industries.

6. Freeman, "Chemical Process Plant."

7. For example, the insurance arrangements of the Exports Credit Guarantee Department, which British-based contractors use for plant and equipment sold overseas, generally require at least 85 percent procurement in the United Kingdom to qualify for coverage. See Freeman, "Chemical Process Plant."

8. Some examples of the links between financial groups and engineering firms are the Banque de Paris et des Pays-Bas, which holds a majority of the equity in Heurtey and Omnium Technique Holding (OTH); Cie. Financière de l'Union Européenne, which has

links with Société pour l'Equipement de l'Industrie Chimique (SPEICHIM); Banque National de Paris and Hambros Bank, which joined with Promochim Ltd., an engineering group, to create Lidechin A. G. (Switzerland) to undertake studies for petrochemical firms.

9. The small size of many of the subsamples in this and subsequent analyses of available data meant that it was often not possible to test the significance of relationships between variables using the Chi-square method. (Many of the cells in tables 2-2 through 2-6 contain less than five observations.) We have instead used the Goodman and Kruskal Tau A and Tau B tests, which indicate the reduction in the error of predicting one variable when the other is known (Hubert M. Blalock, *Social Statistics*, 2d ed. [New York: McGraw-Hill, 1972]).

10. Examples of such arrangements are two Argentine companies, Petrosur Saic and Petroquimica Argentina; Techint (Italy) has a 7 percent holding in the first, and Fish International (United States) has a 15 percent shareholding in the second. Both these foreign shareholders are nonproducers.

11. C. Vaitsos, "Transfer of Industrial Technology to Developing Countries through Private Enterprises," study for the Board of the Cartagena Agreement (Lima and Bogotá, February 1970; processed).

12. For example, both the Belgian Solvay Group and Koppers, a U.S. firm, set up plants in Brazil for the manufacture of final products (PVC and polystyrene respectively) in the 1940s and 1950s; subsequently, they formed joint ventures which sold needed intermediate products to the final producers whom they controlled.

13. P. Gabriel, "The International Transfer of Corporate Skills—Management Contracts in Developing Countries," Division of Research, Harvard University Graduate School of Business Administration, 1967; quoted in C. M. Cooper and F. Sercovitch, *The Channels and Mechanisms for the Transfer of Technology from Developed to Developing Countries*, TR/B/AC 11/5 (Geneva: UNCTAD, April 1971).

14. Ibid.

15. For example, under a management contract to produce synthetic rubber signed in 1961 between a U.S. technology owner and a firm owned by Brazilian public and private shareholders, the technology owner charged an initial lump sum of $650,000 and royalties of 0.6 cent per pound of rubber produced. The management contract established an additional royalty payment in the first year of 0.5 cent per pound of rubber produced over and above 500 tons, or payment of $100,000, whichever was greater. After the first year, the annual rate was fixed at $10,000 per month or 0.5 cent per pound, whichever was greater. In this case it appears that the management contract was used not only to obtain control but also to realize additional royalty payments.

16. The duration of technology agreements has been limited to five years in the Andean Pact countries, but this limitation has not been universally welcomed by recipients. Officials of the Venezuelan Institute of Petroleum, for example, consider that technology agreements should run for ten rather than five years so that recipients can benefit from the technological improvements made by fellow licensees. If recipients consider long-term contracts convenient, regulations limiting the length of the contracts may be by-passed by informal agreements among the parties involved. (See Punto Focal Nacional de Venezuela, "Estudios Sobre Proyectos de Inversión," paper presented to a working meeting of the chemical and petrochemical sector, sponsored by the Organization of American States, Quito, April 1979.)

17. Export restrictions were found in thirty-four out of forty licensing contracts for the production of chemicals and in four out of six contracts for the production of oil and coal derivatives in Chile. (See UNCTAD, "Principales Cuestiones que Plantea la Transmisión de Tecnología: Estudio Monográfico sobre Chile," TD/B/AC.11/20, Geneva, May 1974.)

Chapter 3

The Petrochemical Industry in Latin America: The Recipients

Any contractual arrangement must strike a balance between the interests and relative strengths of the parties involved. The previous chapter has shown something of the nature and contractual preferences of those on the supply side of transfers of petrochemical technology to Latin America; this chapter turns to the recipients. It briefly describes the overall structure of capacity of the petrochemical industry in the seven Latin American countries for which data were collected, outlines the main characteristics of their relevant regulations and local producer groups, and concludes with a discussion of indigenous technological capabilities. Each of these sets of features of the demand side of the transfer process plays a part in shaping the terms and conditions under which transfers take place.

Structure of Capacity

The structure of capacity of the petrochemical industry in Latin America is linked to a number of factors, including the length of time a given country has been producing petrochemicals, the size of the domestic market for a given country's output, opportunities for exporting, and the local availability of raw materials. These factors are also likely to have a bearing on the particular contractual arrangements entered into for the technology transfers on which local production is based. For example, it is reasonable to believe that countries which have built up relatively large petrochemical industries over a long period are likely to have developed some degree of indigenous technical expertise. They may therefore be able to negotiate transfer arrangements which include relatively extensive local participation in pre-start-up activities and license agreements governing post-start-up operations which favor local interests—as opposed to highly packaged transfers of pre-start-up technology or a significant degree of supplier involvement in post-start-up operations. On the other hand, these countries may have acquired a large number of relatively small and inefficient plants in earlier years or have entered into a disproportionately large number of relatively restrictive contracts with suppliers who are producers. (As demonstrated empirically earlier in table 2-6, the technology for older plants has usually been supplied by producers who tend to take a significant ownership share in the recipient entity.)

Recipient entities in countries with relatively large local markets or readily available local sources of raw materials are likely to be in a stronger bargaining position with suppliers. They are therefore able to negotiate relatively unrestricted and unpackaged transfers, if they so wish. Countries whose output capacity is strongly biased toward basic products, or whose plants for manufacturing intermediates are still in the planning or engineering stages, should also have a large proportion of transfers based on relatively unrestricted licensing arrangements. As shown in the empirical data on the sources of transfer in chapter 2, these subsectors tend to be dominated by nonproducer suppliers who are uninterested in restrictive licensing or significant ownership shares in recipient entities. By contrast, countries whose capacity is biased toward final products are likely to have more extensive foreign ownership because, as shown in chapter 2, producers almost completely dominate transfers in this subsector.

Thus, an examination of the structure of output of petrochemicals— the size of existing and planned capacity, the breakdown of that capacity by type of product, and the relative age of plants in different countries— may throw light on the basic issue addressed here: the types of contractual arrangements whereby petrochemical technology is transferred in Latin America and the factors determining them.

Recipient countries' market characteristics vary considerably. Some countries, such as Argentina, Brazil, and Mexico, have been producing petrochemicals for about thirty years, while Chile and more especially Peru have had relatively little experience in the field. Venezuela has the advantage of easily available raw material but only a small home market; if it is to have high-capacity, fully utilized petrochemical production facilities, it must look to exports for the sale of a significant proportion of total output. Brazil is in the opposite position: it has a large domestic market but must rely on imports for its raw materials. Mexico has both a large domestic market and locally available raw material; Chile has neither.

Countries also differ in their levels of protection, the legal conditions of technology transfers and foreign ownership of productive facilities, the extent of state involvement in production, local technical ability, and so on. These questions will be discussed later in this chapter; this section will try to establish quantified intercountry variations in existing and planned capacity by product group, based on survey data collected in 1976 for the seven-country sample. Because of the long time frame for the realization of petrochemical projects, the data probably give a reasonable picture of on-stream operational capacity in the early 1980s. The tabular information covers 275 of the 280 plants which formed the data base (the remaining five had either closed or were unable to supply detailed information). The detailed material from which the summary information by country and product group in this section is drawn will be found in Appendix A.

Basic Products

Table 3-1 provides summary data on basic products by country. In terms of existing plants manufacturing basic products at the time of the survey, Brazil was in first place with 17 plants (30 percent of the total) followed by Argentina with 13 (23 percent) and Mexico with 11 (19 percent). The remaining four countries (Colombia, Venezuela, Chile, and Peru) had a combined total of 16 plants in all, of which six, or nearly half, were in Colombia.

Mexico had the largest existing output capacity, 1,262 thousand metric tons a year, or 28 percent of the total. Brazil (with 1,063 thousand metric tons a year, or 23 percent of total capacity) and Venezuela (with 993 thousand metric tons a year, or 22 percent) were fairly close behind. Venezuela's capacity was based on only four plants; its average plant size (248 thousand metric tons a year) was therefore very much higher than that of Mexico or Brazil (114 thousand metric tons a year per plant and only 62 thousand metric tons a year, respectively). Together these three countries accounted for nearly three-quarters of the 4,531 thousand metric tons a year of existing basic petrochemical capacity in the seven-country group at the time.

In terms of the projected structure of capacity, Brazil again expected to have the largest number of plants by the end of the decade. With five plants in the engineering stage, its share of the total number of plants was expected to be about 29 percent. Mexico, with seven plants in the engineering stage, was expected to have 18 plants, or 24 percent of the total, by the end of the decade. Argentina, with one plant in the engineering stage, was expected to account for 18 percent of all plants.

In the case of projected output capacity, Mexico (with 3,634 thousand metric tons a year, or 37 percent of total projected capacity) was again expected to be the leading producer. Brazil (with 2,025 thousand metric tons a year, or 21 percent) and Venezuela (with 1,761 thousand metric tons a year, or 18 percent) were again in second and third place. The three countries' combined capacity would thus remain at about three-quarters

Table 3-1. *Actual and Future Capacity of 76 Petrochemical Plants for Basic Products, 1976*

| | Existing | | | | Engineering and under construction | | | | Planning | |
| | Plants | | Capacity | | Plants | | Capacity | | Plants | |
Country	Num-ber	Per-cent	Thousand metric tons a year	Per-cent	Num-ber	Per-cent	Thousand metric tons a year	Per-cent	Num-ber	Per-cent
Argentina	13	23	460	10	1	8	400[a]	11	0	0
Brazil	17	30	1,063	23	5	38	962[a]	26	0	0
Chile	3	5	110	2	0	0	0	0	1	17
Colombia	6	11	505	11	0	0	11[a]	0.3	1	17
Mexico	11	19	1,262	28	7	54	2,372	63	0	0
Peru	3	5	138	3	0	0	0	0	2	33
Venezuela	4	7	993	22	0	0	0	0	2	33
Total	57	100	4,531	100	13	100	3,745	100	6	100

Country	Planning Capacity — Thousand metric tons a year	Planning Capacity — Per-cent	Subtotal: future capacity — Plants — Number	Subtotal: future capacity — Plants — Per-cent	Subtotal: future capacity — Capacity — Thousand metric tons a year	Subtotal: future capacity — Capacity — Per-cent	Total: existing and future — Plants — Number	Total: existing and future — Plants — Per-cent	Total: existing and future — Capacity — Thousand metric tons a year	Total: existing and future — Capacity — Per-cent
Argentina	43[a]	3	1	5	443	8	14	18	903	9
Brazil	0	0	5	26	962	18	22	29	2,025	21
Chile	330	22	1	5	330	6	4	9	440	6
Colombia	100	7	1	5	111	2	7	5	616	5
Mexico	0	0	7	37	2,372	45	18	24	3,634	37
Peru	255	17	2	11	255	5	5	7	393	4
Venezuela	768	51	2	11	768	15	6	8	1,761	18
Total	1,496	100	19	100	5,241	100	76	100	9,772	100

Note: All percentages represent proportions of relevant column totals; items may not add to totals because of rounding.
a. Expansion of existing plant.

71

of total projected capacity, but Mexico's share was expected to increase quite significantly, while Brazil's and Venezuela's were projected to decline slightly. Among the smaller producers, Chile was planning to quadruple its capacity through the addition of a single new plant, while Peru was expected nearly to treble its capacity with the addition of two plants to the three in operation in 1976. Total output by all seven countries was projected to be 9,772 thousand metric tons a year, or more than double its 1976 level, by the end of the decade.

Given this sharp expansion in capacity and the predominance of engineering firms and process developers as sources of technology in this subsector, one might expect the number of straight license agreements (the preferred contractual arrangement for this supplier group) to increase in a similar way. The data clearly show, however, that the trend is toward much larger plant capacity in the basics subsector. For the seven-country sample as a whole, average existing capacity was about 79.5 thousand metric tons a year; plants in the engineering and planning stages were expected to have an average capacity of nearly 276 thousand metric tons a year, producing an average for all existing and planned plants of 128.6 thousand metric tons a year. Thus, the total capacity increase was expected to be achieved by a relatively small increase in number of plants (and therefore in number of transfer agreements). The trend toward straight license agreements is therefore likely to be less strong than the figure for tonnage increases alone might suggest.

Intermediate Products

Table 3-2 summarizes the survey information for intermediates. In terms of existing plants, Mexico and Brazil each accounted for 22 plants, or 27 percent of the total number of plants in operation at the time when the data were collected, followed by Argentina (with 14 plants, or 17 percent of the total) and Colombia (with 11, or 14 percent). The remaining three countries, Venezuela, Chile, and Peru, had only 15 percent of the total between them, of which Venezuela had the largest share—10 percent. In terms of existing output capacity, Venezuela alone accounted for 1,098 thousand metric tons a year, or about 32 percent of total capacity for all seven countries, followed by Mexico (with 973 thousand metric tons a year, or 28 percent) and Brazil (with 574 thousand metric tons a year, or 17 percent). As in the case of basic products these three countries accounted for the lion's share of total output—77 percent.

Thus a common pattern appears to be emerging for basic and intermediate products, in which Mexico, Brazil, and Venezuela (in that order) overwhelmingly dominate the scene in terms of tonnage, with

Venezuela having by far the biggest plants, followed by Mexico. In terms of number of plants, Brazil, Mexico, and Argentina (in that order) were the clear leaders in both subsectors. Despite its large number of plants producing both basic and intermediate products, Argentina nevertheless ranked very low in terms of tonnage; it accounted for 10 percent of the seven countries' combined capacity in the case of basics and only 8 percent in the case of intermediates.

The sharp contrast between Venezuela and Argentina—the former with a few plants and large average capacities, and the latter with many plants and small average capacities—is of some interest. Among other things, it may reflect the relatively minor role played in Argentina's petrochemical industry by state enterprises, which, as noted in chapter 2, are virtually the only local entities capable of raising the funds required for large plants. (The participation of state enterprises in the petrochemical industry in Latin America is discussed later in this chapter.)

Other factors which differentiate Argentina and Venezuela are that Argentina entered the petrochemicals field early, when plant capacities generally were relatively small, whereas Venezuela entered later and has plentiful raw materials, which make economies of scale feasible. Table 3-3 gives data on the age structure of the full 280-plant sample by country, showing periods of construction for plants built up to 1975 and stages of realization for those not yet constructed. Nearly three-quarters of all Argentina's plants (operational and projected in 1976) were in existence before 1970; the comparable figure for Venezuela was only one-third.

Size of plant alone, of course, is not necessarily synonymous with efficiency of production, and Venezuela's experience has been far from happy.[1] Nevertheless, Argentina's output structure, embodying a large number of older, low-capacity plants, is also clearly disadvantageous to its petrochemical industry. Moreover, it is likely that Argentina will have a larger share than Venezuela of contracts involving foreign ownership or participation in post-start-up operations, since producers tend to account for a relatively larger share of transfers of technology for intermediate products in the early years.

As shown in table 3-2, Brazil was expected to have the largest number of plants producing intermediates by the end of the 1970s (33, or 28 percent), followed by Mexico (30, or 25 percent) and Argentina (21, or 18 percent). In terms of projected output capacity, both Mexico and Brazil were expected to overtake Venezuela, with projected capacities of 1,904 thousand metric tons a year and 1,696 thousand metric tons a year, respectively (representing 29 percent and 26 percent of total projected capacity) compared with Venezuela's projected 1,150 thousand metric tons a year (18 percent). These three countries together were expected to

Table 3-2. Actual and Future Capacity of 118 Petrochemical Plants for Intermediate Products, 1976

| | Existing | | | | Engineering and under construction | | | | Planning | |
| | Plants | | Capacity | | Plants | | Capacity | | Plants | |
Country	Num-ber	Per-cent	Thousand metric tons a year	Per-cent	Num-ber	Per-cent	Thousand metric tons a year	Per-cent	Num-ber	Per-cent
Argentina	14	17	284	8	2	13	136	8	5	24
Brazil	22	27	574	17	7	44	808	49	4	19
Chile	3	4	43	1	0	0	0	0	2	10
Colombia	11	14	292	9	1	6	16	1	1	5
Mexico	22	27	973	28	5	31	631	38	3	14
Peru	1	1	168	5	0	0	0	0	6	29
Venezuela	8	10	1,098	32	1	6	52	3	0	0
Total	81	100	3,432	100	16	100	1,643	100	21	100

| Country | Planning Capacity | | Subtotal: future capacity | | | | Total: existing and future | | | |
	Thousand metric tons a year	Per-cent	Plants Number	Per-cent	Capacity Thousand metric tons a year	Per-cent	Plants Number	Per-cent	Capacity Thousand metric tons a year	Per-cent
Argentina	191	13	7	19	327	11	21	18	611	9
Brazil	314	23	11	30	1,122	36	33	28	1,696	26
Chile	325	23	2	5	325	10	5	4	368	6
Colombia	50	3	2	5	66	2	13	11	358	5
Mexico	300	21	8	22	931	30	30	25	1,904	29
Peru	257	18	6	16	257	8	7	6	425	7
Venezuela	0	0	1	3	52	1	9	8	1,150	18
Total	1,437	100	37	100	3,080	100	118	100	6,512	100

Note: All percentages represent proportions of relevant column totals; items may not add to totals because of rounding.

Table 3-3. *Period of Construction and Stage of the Project: 280 Petrochemical Plants*
(number)

Country	Constructed					Engineering and under construc-tion	Plan-ning	Closed and un-known	Total
	Pre-1960	1960–69	1970–75	Date un-known	Sub-total				
Argentina	9	28	3	0	40	4	6	1	51
Brazil	11	16	17	8	52	20	6	2	80
Colombia	0	14	4	6	24	2	2	0	28
Chile	1	3	5	0	9	0	4	0	13
Mexico	2	28	6	12	48	13	5	2	68
Peru	0	3	2	0	5	0	14	0	19
Venezuela	0	7	8	0	15	2	4	0	21
Total	23	99	45	26	193	41	41	5	280

account for 73 percent of total future capacity—a slight reduction from their 77 percent share in the seven-country total in 1976.

As in the case of basic products, projections for intermediates show a pattern of increasing average plant capacity, although the average increase for plants being engineered or planned was much less dramatic than that for basic products. For all seven countries as a group, the average capacity of plants in existence in 1976 was just over 43 thousand metric tons a year, while that for plants being engineered or planned was about 59 thousand metric tons a year. Average capacity for all plants, existing and planned, was just over 55 thousand metric tons a year. Countries with particularly high average capacities for plants being engineered or planned were Chile (162.5 thousand metric tons a year for an admittedly small sample of two plants), followed by Mexico (just over 116 thousand metric tons a year for eight projected plants) and Brazil (102 thousand metric tons a year for 11 plants being engineered or planned).

Final Products

Table 3-4 shows the breakdown for final products. This subsector was clearly dominated by Brazil, which had 13 existing plants (24 percent of all plants in operation in 1976) with a combined capacity of 512 thousand metric tons a year (43 percent of total existing capacity). Mexico (with 27 percent of existing plants and 20 percent of total capacity) and Argentina (with 24 percent of total number of plants and 20 percent of capacity) were next in importance. The remaining four countries together accounted for only 25 percent of existing plants for final products and for just 17 percent of capacity. In terms of projected number of plants and output capacity, Brazil was expected to increase its lead further, accounting for nearly 40 percent of the 26 new plants being engineered or planned in 1976, and over one-third (562 thousand metric tons a year) of all projected new capacity (1,663 thousand metric tons a year).

Plants being engineered or planned were projected to raise output by nearly 150 percent, but the number of new plants was projected to rise by only about 50 percent. Thus, while plant capacity was in general much smaller for final products than for basic or intermediate products, there was, as in the other subgroups, a significant projected increase in average plant capacity—from just under 22 thousand metric tons a year for those existing in 1976 to nearly 64 thousand metric tons a year for those being engineered or planned. Interestingly, Mexico had the lowest average capacity level for existing plants (15.9 thousand metric tons a year) and

Table 3-4. *Actual and Future Capacity of 81 Petrochemical Plants for Final Products, 1976*

| | Existing | | | | Engineering and under construction | | | | Planning | |
| | Plants | | Capacity | | Plants | | Capacity | | Plants | |
Country	Num-ber	Per-cent	Thousand metric tons a year	Per-cent	Num-ber	Per-cent	Thousand metric tons a year	Per-cent	Num-ber	Per-cent
Argentina	13	24	242	20	1	8	85	13	1	7
Brazil	13	24	512	43	8	67	412	62	2	14
Chile	3	5	41	3	0	0	0	0	1	7
Colombia	7	13	88	7	1	8	58	9	0	0
Mexico	15	27	239	20	1	8	40	6	2	14
Peru	1	2	7	1	0	0	0	0	6	43
Venezuela	3	5	74	6	1	8	70	11	2	14
Total	55	100	1,203	100	12	100	665	100	14	100

Country	Planning		Subtotal: future capacity				Total: existing and future			
	Capacity		Plants		Capacity		Plants		Capacity	
	Thousand metric tons a year	Per-cent	Num-ber	Per-cent	Thousand metric tons a year	Per-cent	Num-ber	Per-cent	Thousand metric tons a year	Per-cent
Argentina	60	6	2	8	145	9	15	19	387	14
Brazil	150	15	10	38	562	34	23	28	1,074	37
Chile	50	5	1	4	50	3	4	5	91	3
Colombia	0	0	1	4	58	3	8	10	146	5
Mexico	280	28	3	12	320	19	18	22	559	20
Peru	288	29	6	23	288	17	7	9	295	10
Venezuela	170	17	3	12	240	14	6	7	314	11
Total	998	100	26	100	1,663	100	81	100	2,866	100

Note: All percentages represent proportions of relevant column totals; items may not add to totals because of rounding.

79

the highest average capacity level for projected plants (nearly 107 thousand metric tons a year).

It will be recalled from chapter 2 that the technology for plants producing final products is almost wholly supplied by producer companies, and that this supplier group tends to prefer contractual arrangements which give them an equity share or control of some other kind over recipients' post-start-up operations. Since Argentina and Mexico, and especially Brazil, dominate the output of final products, it might be expected that these countries would show an above average degree of foreign participation in their petrochemical industries. The structure of participation in different countries is discussed in the next section.

Summary and Conclusion

The data show the overwhelming predominance of one group of countries (Argentina, Brazil, and Mexico) in the number of plants, and of a second group (Brazil, Mexico, and Venezuela) in output capacity. Brazil has the largest number of plants in all three product group categories; Mexico has the largest output capacity in basic and intermediate products, while Brazil has the largest capacity in final products. Venezuela has the highest overall average plant capacity of the four countries (taking all three product categories together), and Argentina has the lowest.

It was suggested that the structure of capacity by product group and country may affect the distribution by country of different types of technology transfer agreements. These variables will be linked in the concluding discussion in chapter 4. It was also pointed out, however, that other factors will affect the country-by-country incidence of licensing agreements on the one hand and agreements involving some degree or another of supplier ownership of the recipient entity on the other hand. These factors include the extent to which recipient countries' governments regulate or participate directly in the ownership of petrochemical plants, the relative strength of local public and private groups in the industry, and the degree of local technological development in different countries.

Structure of Participation

As noted in chapter 2, local market characteristics and government policies can affect the contractual arrangements for transfers preferred by suppliers of technology; and although suppliers who are also producers generally prefer to take an ownership position in recipient entities, the arrangements under which technology is in fact transferred range from the use of straight licensing agreements to setting up wholly owned subsidiaries. Moreover, individual suppliers appear to be quite flexible in terms of the arrangements used; the same supplier may transfer technology under different arrangements on different occasions (table 2-10). The subsections which follow outline the variations in government policy and the structure of participation from country to country, in order to throw some light on how these factors influence the different arrangements under which technology is transferred.

The Regulatory Framework

The structure of participation in the petrochemical industry in Latin America is strongly influenced by the regulatory framework in each country. This framework rests on legislation covering import substitution and market protection and regulations dealing with foreign investment and technology transfer arrangements.

IMPORT SUBSTITUTION AND MARKET PROTECTION. Policies adopted in the past have tended to encourage foreign technology owners to transfer technologies for petrochemical production to Latin American countries. More specifically, import substitution policies have given both suppliers and recipients incentives to set up local plants for manufacturing petrochemicals, which are then fostered by market protection policies. These policies have had some success in building up local petrochemical production capacity in Latin American countries, but this success has not been without its costs. In particular, the structure of market protection policies has tended to be biased in favor of final products—the subsector dominated by foreign technology suppliers who are also producers, the group most likely to take an ownership position in recipient entities. Two factors in particular have fostered this bias: both nominal and effective rates of protection are higher for final than for other products, and government support for plants producing intermediates has led to subsidization of inputs for final products. Meanwhile, efforts directed toward import substitution have led to the construction of plants which are often of suboptimal scale by international standards. The Argentine case was mentioned in the previous section; data comparing plant output capacities in Latin America with developed-country standards are given in Appendix B.

FOREIGN INVESTMENT. In recent years, developing countries in Latin America have become increasingly concerned about the extent of foreign

Table 3-5. *Summary Data on Local and Foreign Participation in Plant Ownership: 280 Petrochemical Plants*

Recipient country	(a) L	(b) F^-	(c) (a)+(b)	(d) L/F	(e) F^+	(f) F	(g) (e)+(f)	(h) (c)+(d)+(g)	(i) F?	(j) ?	(k) (h)+(i)+(j)
Argentina	15	8	23	0	9	18	27	50	0	1	51
Brazil	18	25	43	3	13	17	30	76	2	2	80
Chile	9	0	9	0	3	1	4	13	0	0	13
Colombia	11	1	12	1	2	11	13	26	2	0	28
Mexico	44	13	57	0	0	6	6	63	3	2	68
Peru	17	1	18	0	0	1	1	19	0	0	19
Venezuela	11	9	20	0	0	1	1	21	0	0	21
Total	125	57	182	4	27	55	82	268	7	5	280

Key: L = local participation only; F^- = foreign minority participation; L/F = shared local/foreign participation; F^+ = foreign majority participation; F = subsidiary of foreign firm; F? = foreign participation but extent not known; ? = participation arrangements not known.

investment in their petrochemical industries. Venezuela and Mexico have given state corporations monopolies in the manufacture of basic petrochemicals since the late 1950s and have required that these corporations own a majority of projects for the manufacture of intermediate products. Argentina, Colombia, Chile, and Peru adopted broadly similar policies in the early 1970s. Brazil has not formally limited foreign participation in any subsector, but its state petrochemical enterprise has increasingly participated in projects of any significant size (see next subsection).

Entities manufacturing final products are not regulated by legislation aimed specifically at petrochemicals, but general legislation on foreign investment applies in this sector as in others. For example, foreign participation in new investments in Mexico is limited to a 49 percent shareholding. The "fade out" provisions of the Andean Pact's 1971 Decision 24 include a similar provision for new investment and a requirement that existing firms comply with it within fifteen years. Argentina's General Foreign Investment Law limits profit remission to 12.5 percent a year and requires that foreign participation in any local entity be reduced to a 20 percent shareholding within a fixed timetable.

TECHNOLOGY TRANSFER. In addition to regulating foreign investment, both in the petrochemical industry and more generally, Latin American countries have begun directly to limit certain types of technology transfer. Examples of such restrictions include Decision 24 of the Andean Pact and Mexico's 1972 Law on the Transfer of Technology and the Use and Exploitation of Patents and Trademarks. The latter incorporates very widely ranging provisions, many of them directly addressed to the arrangements for suppliers' influence over recipients' post-start-up operations outlined in chapter 2.[2]

Thus, although there may be variations in the longevity or intensity of individual countries' legislation, the trend in recent years has been toward tightening the regulatory framework and limiting foreign participation in the petrochemical industry. On the basis of the various regulatory frameworks summarized above, one would expect Mexico and Venezuela to have the highest proportion of plants under local ownership, and Brazil to have the lowest. Table 3-5 provides summary data by country on the ownership of the 280 plants surveyed.

Of the plants whose ownership is known (except for the Peruvian and Chilean industries, which have very small shares of total output) Mexico does indeed have by far the largest proportion wholly owned by local interests: 44 out of the country's 63, or 70 percent (column a/h). Of the other relatively large producers, Venezuela's locally owned plants (11 out of 21) put it in second place in this category (52 percent). If plants with total and majority local ownership are combined (column c), Venezuela moves into first place, with 20 out of 21 plants (95 percent) under local control, and Mexico comes second with 57 out of 63, or 91 percent of plants whose ownership is known.

At the other end of the scale, Brazil as predicted has the lowest proportion of wholly locally owned plants out of the total number whose ownership is known (18 out of 76, or 24 percent). Interestingly, however, both Argentina and Colombia have higher proportions of plants under total foreign ownership than Brazil (18 out of 50, or 36 percent, and 11 out of 26, or 42 percent, respectively). If total and majority foreign ownership are combined (column g) a similar pattern persists: Argentina now comes first, with 27 out of 50 plants under foreign control (54 percent), followed by Colombia (13 out of 26, or 50 percent). Brazil is third, with 30 out of the 76 of its plants whose ownership is known under foreign control (40 percent).

A partial explanation for this phenomenon can be found by inspecting the raw data on which table 3-5 is based, which are not reproduced here. Argentina and Colombia were the only countries with a significant proportion of plants producing basic products under foreign ownership (6 out of 14 existing or planned plants, or 43 percent of all plants in this subgroup, in the case of Argentina and 2 out of 7, or 29 percent, in the case of Colombia). Both countries were relatively early starters in the petrochemical industry (see table 3-3); as shown in table 2-6, producers (who favor foreign ownership) had a significantly higher share of transfers of technology for basic products in the years prior to 1970 than in more recent periods. The extent of public participation in the industry is also an important factor: although Brazil does not explicitly restrict foreign ownership, its public enterprise petrochemical corporation, Petroquisa, is an active partner in most important projects.

A time series analysis of the raw data on which table 3-5 is based shows a marked aggregate shift over time toward local ownership. The seven-country total of 125 wholly locally owned plants (column a) is made up of 7 plants completed before 1960, 43 completed between 1960 and 1969, and 74 with post-1970 completion dates; these subtotals represented 30 percent, 43 percent, and 56 percent respectively of all plants in these three time categories. A similar pattern is evident over time for plants with local majority ownership. This trend toward local control of petrochemical plants in Latin America reflects conditions in the recipient countries, including the increasingly rigorous regulatory framework just described.

Participant Groups

The simplified picture of the structure of ownership in the 280 plants in table 3-5 showed a pattern of ownership broadly related to the regulatory framework in the principal recipient countries. This simplified picture, however, conceals a large number of different ownership arrangements. Table 3-6 shows the range of participatory combinations of three groups—local public enterprises (denoted by G in the table), local private industrial and financial groups (denoted by L in the table), and foreign firms (denoted by F in the table)—with varying degrees of local and foreign ownership.

Apart from the many permutations of participation which the table reveals, perhaps the most interesting point is the very extensive role of public enterprises. Of the 268 plants whose ownership structure was known, state corporations participated to a greater or lesser degree in 103 of the 125 plants under total local ownership (82 percent), 39 of the 57 plants with majority local ownership (68 percent), 1 of the 4 plants with fifty-fifty local/foreign ownership (25 percent), and 10 of the 27 plants with majority foreign ownership (37 percent). By product type (again taking only the 268 plants whose ownership was known), public enterprises participated in 56 of the 77 plants manufacturing basic products (73 percent), 66 of the 117 intermediate plants (56 percent), and 31 of the 74 plants manufacturing final products (42 percent). Overall, public enterprises participated in the ownership of 153 of the 268 plants whose ownership was known, or over 57 percent of the total.

This very high participation rate by state enterprises reflects the national legislation outlined in the previous subsection. In addition, foreign suppliers of technology may see some degree of government participation as a form of insurance which reduces the financial and political risks attached to their own stake in project entities. In some countries, where local private enterprises are relatively small in scale and lack the funds to take equity holdings in petrochemical plants, state enterprises may be the only local partners available (the table shows 17 pure state/foreign joint ventures out of the 88 local/foreign partnerships whose composition was known, or nearly 20 percent of all joint ventures). The respective roles of the three participant groups in the seven-country sample are briefly discussed below.

STATE ENTERPRISES. State enterprises, operating as sole owners of petrochemical plants or in partnership with local and foreign private firms,

Table 3-6. *Participation Structure, by Type of Product:*
280 Petrochemical Plants

Participation structure	Type of product			
	Basic	Intermediate	Final	Total
Local				
G	42	40	13	95
G$^+$L	1	0	2	3
G/L	1	1	0	2
GL$^+$	1	1	1	3
L	3	17	2	22
Subtotal	48	59	18	125
Majority local				
JVGF$^-$	3	5	2	10
JV(G$^+$L)F$^-$	6	1	2	9
JVG/LF$^-$	0	0	1	1
JV(GL$^+$)F$^-$	1	7	3	11
JV(GL)F$^-$	1	4	3	8
JVLF$^-$	1	7	10	18
Subtotal	12	24	21	57
Joint				
JVG/F	0	0	1	1
JVL/F	1	0	2	3
Subtotal	1	0	3	4
Majority foreign				
JVGF$^+$	0	4	2	6
JV(G$^+$L)F$^+$	0	2	1	3
JV(GL)F$^+$	0	1	0	1
JVLF$^+$	5	8	4	17
Subtotal	5	15	7	27
Foreign				
F	11	19	25	55
Subtotal	11	19	25	55
Not known				
JVF?	0	1	6	7
?	0	2	3	5
Subtotal	0	3	9	12
Total	77	120	83	280

Key: JV = joint venture; G = public enterprises; L = local private firms; F = foreign firms; + = majority participation; − = minority participation; / = equal participation; ? = unknown.

have a relatively long history in Latin America. Such enterprises are of particular importance in Mexico and Brazil. Mexico's principal state petrochemicals enterprise, Pemex, is in charge of oil production and plays a dominant role in the petrochemical industry. Pemex was created in 1938 and began manufacturing petrochemicals in the late 1950s. By 1973 it owned petrochemical complexes at ten sites, manufacturing more than thirty different products. Pemex also participates in joint ventures with local and foreign private firms for the manufacture of downstream products derived from the basic products it manufactures in its own plants. The other large Mexican state enterprise, Guanos y Fertilizantes de México (GUANOMEX) operates in the fertilizers subsector. Founded in 1943, GUANOMEX now controls about 96 percent of Mexico's fertilizer production.

Pemex has used its position in the petrochemical industry to foster the development of local capabilities in the fields of equipment manufacturing, detailed engineering, and even basic engineering. (Local capacity to undertake these and other elements of pre-start-up activities will be discussed in more detail in the last section of this chapter.)

In Brazil, oil and gas production is in the hands of Petroleos Brasileiros (Petrobras), formed in 1954. In 1968 Petrobras set up Petroquisa, a state enterprise designed to participate with local and foreign private firms in petrochemical production. By 1974 Petroquisa had stakes in more than twenty petrochemical companies.

Unlike Pemex, Petroquisa only rarely operates as sole owner of the plants in whose ownership it participates. Its ownership arrangements are of three broad kinds. In very large projects (involving average investments of over US $200 million), Petroquisa has taken a majority position, allowing foreign investors only a small proportion of total equity. In medium-size investments (averaging about US $50 million), the equity is split roughly equally between Petroquisa, local private interests, and foreign firms, with Petroquisa's share being equal to or larger than that of the foreign partner in all cases. A third type of arrangement is used for small investments, averaging under US $20 million, in which Petroquisa holds only a minority share and encourages local private firms to hold the majority of the equity.[3]

In Argentina, Yacimentos Petrolíferos Fiscales (YPF) has controlled the exploration, development, and marketing of oil and natural gas since the 1920s; it set up the first petrochemical plant in Latin America in 1943. In 1951, another state enterprise, Dirección General de Fabricaciones Militares (DGFM), began to produce aromatics at a plant near Buenos Aires. Despite the early involvement of the Argentine government in petrochemical production, its overall participation in the industry remained relatively low until 1973, when the production of basic petrochemicals was reserved to the state. As table 3-5 shows, foreign ownership or majority participation in petrochemical projects in Argentina remains relatively high.

In Venezuela, by contrast with Mexico, Brazil, and Argentina, oil refineries were initially controlled by international oil companies. The Venezuelan state petrochemical enterprise, the Venezuelan Institute of Petrochemicals (IVP), was created in 1956 and started operations in the petrochemical field in 1963 with a fertilizer complex at Morón. As of 1976, when the survey data were collected, IVP had participated or was planning to participate in a series of joint ventures with local and foreign firms. Five of these ventures had started production between 1969 and 1973, five others were in the engineering or construction stages, and six more were settled in principle but were awaiting government approval and the selection of a foreign partner. IVP's participation in joint ventures varies from 10 to 75 percent, but IVP and local partners together usually own 50 percent or more of the equity.

The remaining three countries also have state petrochemical enterprises, but their activities are on a much smaller scale than those described above. Colombia's Ecopetrol, founded in 1967, has bought out a number of enterprises which were formerly owned by foreign firms. Chile's state enterprise, Petroquimica Chilena, was set up in 1966 and is a minority partner in one joint venture with a foreign firm (Dow). In Peru, where the petrochemical industry is almost entirely in local hands, two state enterprises, Petroleos del Perú and Induperu, operate and promote petrochemical complexes in Talara and Vayovar respectively.

LOCAL PRIVATE GROUPS. The relatively few local private groups participating in the ownership of petrochemical plants in Latin America fall into two categories. The first is made up of chemical firms which started by producing other materials and later jointed state enterprises or foreign firms in petrochemical projects, usually for the production of intermediates they had previously imported. The other category is composed of financial holding companies formed to promote (usually in association with a state enterprise) the development of the petrochemical industry. The few local groups active in the sector tend to participate in several projects at the same time.

Local private participation in the petrochemical industry is most evident in Brazil, where both chemical companies and financial holding companies have shares in a relatively large number of plants in association with Petroquisa or foreign firms, including three of the four fifty-fifty partnerships in our 280-plant sample. In addition, as noted in chapter 2,

Brazilian development banks have participated in the financing and ownership of petrochemical projects. Argentina also has a significant degree of local ownership, but local shareholdings are relatively widely diffused (unlike the Brazilian pattern where they are concentrated in a few companies). This probably reflects the fact that Argentina's capital market is relatively highly developed compared with those of other Latin American countries. In Venezuela, two local groups are involved in several joint ventures with IVP; three other local producers have minority holdings in a number of joint ventures. Mexico's most important local producer, Celulosa y Derivados, participates with smaller local associates in three joint ventures with foreign firms; in all three cases, Celulosa y Derivados holds a majority of the shares.

FOREIGN FIRMS. For the purpose of this analysis, the term "foreign firms" relates to producers only—that is, oil and chemical companies—since nonproducer companies almost never participate in the ownership of local petrochemical companies to which they transfer technology. Where government regulations of long standing reserve the manufacture of, say, basic petrochemicals to the state, foreign companies' participation will be effectively confined to intermediate and final products, either as sole owners of plants or as partners with local public or private enterprises. Where such restrictions do not exist or are of recent origin, foreign firms may also participate in the manufacture of basic products (Argentina is a case in point). If the local partner commands sufficiently large resources, foreign firms will usually participate in an entity through capitalization of royalties (see chapter 2). This procedure may not be feasible where local partners are relatively weak in financial terms; in these cases, the foreign partner will need to invest directly in the local entity.

As noted earlier, Argentina and Colombia have the largest proportion of plants wholly owned by foreign interests or with foreign majority holdings. In the case of Argentina the main influx occurred after a 1958 foreign investment law offered major incentives to overseas investors. Seventy-five percent of all firms in Argentina's petrochemical industry were established during the 1960s;[4] by the end of the decade, affiliates of U.S. corporations alone accounted for approximately 30 percent of total sales in the industry.[5] Foreign participation permeated all three subsectors (basic, intermediate, and final products), and the contractual arrangements mainly took the form of majority or sole foreign ownership of plants. Six out of thirteen plants producing basic petrochemicals in Argentina in the early 1970s were wholly owned subsidiaries of foreign firms, and two more had majority foreign ownership. Of the thirteen plants producing intermediates early in the decade, five were wholly owned subsidiaries and another three had majority foreign participation. Since 1973, however, when Argentina passed legislation restricting foreign ownership, the ownership of some of these plants has reverted to local majority control. Colombia has a similar pattern of initial foreign dominance of the industry, mainly through wholly owned subsidiaries, followed recently by a trend toward local acquisition of ownership.

As already noted, Brazil has the lowest proportion of plants wholly owned by local interests, but comes third after Argentina and Colombia in its share of wholly or mainly foreign-owned entities. In fact, of all seven countries under study, Brazil appears to have the most balanced participation structure: a strong state enterprise, a significant degree of local private participation, and foreign ownership arrangements covering the whole spectrum from wholly owned subsidiaries to straight licensing agreements with no foreign participation. Since the foundation of Petroquisa in 1968, however, foreign participation has increasingly taken the form of minority shareholdings in partnership with Petroquisa and local private groups. Despite this trend toward local control, foreign firms still accounted for 51 percent of the total capital invested in the Brazilian petrochemical industry as late as 1973. By 1976 (see Appendix A) 12 out of Brazil's 22 plants for producing basic products had foreign participation and 3 of these were wholly owned subsidiaries of foreign firms. Of the country's 33 intermediate plants, 25 had foreign participation of which 7 were wholly owned subsidiaries. All but one of Brazil's 23 plants manufacturing final products had some degree of foreign participation; 8 were wholly owned subsidiaries.

Foreign firms are also active in Mexico despite long-standing legislation that restricts their participation to final and some intermediate products. By the end of the 1960s, foreign capital represented 35 percent of total investment in the Mexican petrochemical industry.[6] The extent of foreign control, however, was very slight; the data in Appendix A show that only 3 of the 18 plants for manufacturing final products, one of the 30 intermediate plants, and none of the 18 plants for basic products were wholly owned subsidiaries; a further 3 plants for manufacturing final products were majority foreign-owned. The small Chilean and Peruvian industries also have relatively low levels of foreign participation, except in the case of plants manufacturing final products in Chile (for details, see Appendix A).

Table 2-10 provided a breakdown by supplier of the varying degrees of participation in 127 plants, 124 of which used technology supplied by a foreign producer. The table showed that individual firms could be relatively flexible in their contractual arrangements for transfers; the same

Table 3-7. *Foreign Producer Firms' Participation in the Petrochemical Industry in Latin America, by Country of Origin: 124 Petrochemical Plants*
(number)

Country of origin	Firms	Agree-ments	Type of participation							Total
			L	F^-	L/F	F^+	F	F?	?	
United States	26	64	13	17	2	10	19	3	0	64
Germany, Fed. Rep. of	5	12	4	2	0	1	5	0	0	12
France	4	9	3	3	0	1	2	0	0	9
United Kingdom	2	9	4	4	0	0	1	0	0	9
Italy	1	8	7	1	0	0	0	0	0	8
Japan	5	7	4	3	0	0	0	0	0	7
Belgium	2	4	1	1	0	0	2	0	0	4
Netherlands	1	4	0	4	0	0	0	0	0	4
Netherlands and United Kingdom	1	2	1	0	0	0	0	0	1	2
Sweden	1	3	3	0	0	0	0	0	0	3
Austria	1	1	1	0	0	0	0	0	0	1
Canada	1	1	0	1	0	0	0	0	0	1
Total	50	124	41	36	2	12	29	3	1	124

Key: L = local participation only; F^- = foreign minority participation; L/F = shared local/foreign participation; F^+ = foreign majority participation; F = subsidiary of foreign firm; F? = foreign participation but extent not known; ? = participation arrangements not known.

firm might have total control in some cases and minimal or no control (at least in terms of equity participation) in others. Table 3-7 presents an overview of the data for the 124 plants whose technology was provided by foreign suppliers. It shows the number of firms and transfer agreements in each case, together with the distribution of agreements by the degree of supplier participation specified.

U.S. producers represent by far the largest source of transfers, with 26 out of the total of 50 supplier firms (52 percent) and 64 out of the 124 transfer agreements (also 52 percent). In terms of number of agreements, West Germany is next with 12, or nearly 10 percent, followed by the United Kingdom and France with 9 agreements each (7 percent), Italy with 8 (6.5 percent), and Japan with 7 (nearly 6 percent).

Firms originating in the United States also have by far the largest ownership stake in petrochemical projects in Latin America. They account for 19 of the 29 contracts setting up wholly owned subsidiaries (66 percent), 10 of the 12 contracts permitting majority participation (83 percent), and both the contracts identified in table 3-7 as providing for fifty-fifty local/foreign participation. U.S. suppliers also account for the largest proportion of transfers involving total *local* ownership (that is, straight license agreements; 13 out of 41, or 32 percent of this subgroup). But *as a proportion of its total transfers* where the type of agreement is known (13 out of 61, or 21 percent), the United States has fewer agreements of this kind than any other country, except the Netherlands and Canada, which have small samples. If contracts permitting majority local ownership are included, the United States is again the least "liberal" in the proportion of transfer agreements specifying local control (30 out of 61 cases where the type of ownership is known, or 49 percent of all U.S. transfers), although Germany and Belgium are only marginally more willing to permit agreements of this type (with a combined total of 6 out of 12 and 2 out of 4, or 50 percent in each case).

In table 3-8 the twelve most important suppliers (those with four or more transfers each) are ranked by the number of plants to which they have transferred technology. All but one of these suppliers (Phillips Petroleum) were chemical companies, and, as already noted, many of them appeared to pursue fairly flexible policies with regard to transfer. They did not confine themselves to setting up subsidiaries or majority-owned local entities, but also undertook transfers involving minority holdings or straight licensing agreements (see table 2–10).

Summary and Conclusion

The regulatory framework within which production takes place and the relative importance of different groups of participants (state enterprises, local private groups, and foreign firms) vary significantly from country to country. These factors are likely to influence the terms and conditions under which technology is transferred. To the extent that a country has (a) a large local market and a petrochemical industry which has accumulated experience over a relatively long period of time; (b) a regulatory framework and a participation structure which favor local ownership; and (c) a product mix which places relatively low emphasis on final products, there are more likely to be relatively unpackaged contractual arrangements and opportunities for indigenous technological development. Survey data that relate product factors and the contractual arrangements for technology transfers will be analyzed in chapter 4.

Another aspect of the technology transfer process in Latin America that may also have a bearing on the terms and conditions of transfers is the level of technological capability in recipient countries. This is manifested in their ability to bring a project from initial conceptualization to

Table 3-8. *Twelve Most Important Suppliers, by Number of Transfers*

Company	Country	Number of transfers
Dow	United States	8
Montecatini	Italy	8
Koppers	United States	7
Phillips	United States	7
Imperial Chemical Industries	United Kingdom	6
Badische Anilin-und-Soda Fabrik	Germany, Fed. Rep. of	5
Borden	United States	5
Monsanto	United States	5
Diamond Shamrock	United States	4
Goodrich	United States	4
Rhone Poulenc	France	4
Dutch State Mines	Netherlands	4

the moment production begins and their ability to modify and adapt existing technologies imported from abroad. In general, it might be expected that past transfers of technology would have stimulated indigenous technological ability. What kinds of expertise in fact exist, and how are they being deployed?

Local Technological Capabilities

As noted in chapter 1, technology transfers between developed and developing countries typically must bridge a considerable "technological distance" because of the relative imbalance between the technological capabilities of the two groups. The size of this technological distance is a major determinant of the extent to which technology transfers are packaged—and thus of the degree of supplier involvement in pre- and post-start-up activities associated with a given project. This section examines how far the seven Latin American countries studied have narrowed the technological distance by developing indigenous capabilities in the field of petrochemical technology. As the gap between suppliers and recipients becomes smaller, the bargaining strength of a supplier will be reduced—unless the supplier has a monopoly over the process the recipient wants, which is only rarely the case in petrochemicals. Thus, the degree of local technological capability is an important element in the choice of contractual arrangements for technology transfers.

Local technological capability can be analyzed in terms of the elements of technical knowledge required to realize a project, which were outlined in chapter 1. For the purposes of this section, these items are grouped as follows, in ascending order of their complexity:

1. Ability to carry out preinvestment, feasibility, and pre-project technical studies
2. Ability to manufacture machinery and equipment
3. Ability to undertake project management and detailed engineering
4. Ability to undertake basic engineering and process adaptation and development.

Initial Studies

When trying to incorporate local elements into the process of realizing a petrochemical project, the first stage is to develop a domestic capability to carry out prefeasibility and feasibility studies. This capability may be in the hands of local autonomous consultancy firms, industry-linked planning and programming institutes, or the department(s) responsible for project evaluation and technical studies in the firm undertaking the project. Knowledge of local economic and social conditions is essential for selecting, evaluating, and organizing the different elements of the project at the planning stage. As the project advances, those responsible for the initial studies can continue to advise the project owner on technical matters. Engineering firms or the engineering department of the project entity can then use this advice in the later stages of project realization.

Local consultancy firms are in a good position to advise project owners and national planning authorities about alternative production processes and to identify elements (such as civil works, utilities, and off-site activities) that can usually be undertaken locally. Moreover, their familiarity with local conditions may make them better able than foreign firms to estimate sales and costs, and to identify problems of integration with existing plants and other enterprises.[7] The difficulty of getting reliable information about production costs, however, limits opportunities for local execution of feasibility studies in the recipient countries. Some owners of technology are more ready than others to supply this kind of information, but they will usually do so only if the probability of their winning the contract is high.

The indigenous capacity to carry out feasibility and pre-project studies is well developed in the countries in our sample which made an early start in petrochemicals (Mexico, Brazil, and Argentina). In Mexico and Brazil, this capacity is especially concentrated in their respective government enterprises, Pemex and Petroquisa. By contrast, the countries of the Andean subregion are still very much behind in developing local consultancy capability.

Procurement and Equipment Supply

Technology suppliers will usually be willing to use local sources for equipment that is not specific to a process, provided it fully meets the necessary technical specifications. In many cases, such equipment is in fact locally available; as early as 1957, for example, about 20 percent of the equipment needed for the expansion of the Mataripe refinery in Brazil was locally produced.[8] This project marked the start of local production of equipment for the oil refining and petrochemical industry in Brazil.[9] For the next petrochemical project, Brazilian equipment suppliers provided 50 percent of the equipment. Despite this early start, imported equipment accounted for about 53 percent of the total procurement costs of a subsequent project for a large petrochemical center in northeastern Brazil. This state of affairs cannot be explained by the sources of finance, because only 24 percent of the investment was financed through foreign credits. Moreover, the Brazilian authorities have developed a flexible system to finance locally produced capital goods, under which a firm can obtain funds for equipment outside the financing of the project as a whole. These funds may cover up to 90 percent of the price of the equipment: 60 percent of each loan is covered by Banco Nacional de Desenvolvimento Economico (BNDE) and 40 percent by private banks. In the case in question, a more likely explanation of the high proportion of imported equipment is that the basic engineering for the project was undertaken abroad—and the designer naturally specified equipment with which he was most familiar.

In Mexico, Pemex has followed an explicit policy of incorporating locally produced equipment into its plants. Once the engineering of a project is finished, Pemex meets with representatives of Mexican industrial associations to determine what equipment and materials can be locally supplied.[10] In 1973, locally produced machinery and equipment made up about 75 percent of Pemex's procurement.[11] Nevertheless, for certain projects (such as those for the manufacture of ammonia) the local supply of major equipment is limited. Thus, despite a dramatic reduction in Pemex's dependence on external financing from suppliers and contractors (from 1,299 million pesos in 1967 to 154 million pesos in 1974), equipment imports in 1973 were valued at 1,785 million pesos. This is probably because Mexico's capital goods sector is less developed than that of, say, Argentina or Brazil, and its proximity to the United States makes the import of equipment relatively easy.

Argentina purchases locally about the same proportion of equipment and materials as does Mexico. It is estimated that 70 percent of the equipment and materials for the Bahia Blanca complex will be purchased locally; imported items include compressors, turbines, pumps, and measuring instruments.[12]

The tendency toward greater automation in the petrochemical industry places an important new constraint on the use of locally produced equipment in Latin American countries. The growing use of computerized equipment has reinforced links between engineering firms and equipment suppliers in developed countries. This trend has also strengthened the bargaining position of general contractors who are able to offer performance guarantees for all equipment supplied.

In the Andean countries, the petrochemical sectors are generally smaller and newer than those of the major producers, and the local supply of equipment is more limited than in the countries mentioned above. In Venezuela, the supply of local equipment is confined to peripheral elements of projects, and equipment suppliers tend to be associated with foreign firms.[13] This may be in part because the capacity structure of the Venezuelan petrochemical industry is characterized by a small number of relatively large plants. Since 1969, to avoid conflicts of interest, the Department of Mixed Enterprises within IVP has stipulated that partners chosen for mixed enterprises should not be directly or indirectly associated with engineering firms or equipment fabricators, and that construction, assembly, and procurement should be subject to competitive bidding. These conditions are not backed by appropriate legislation, however, and have therefore not been universally followed.

Appendix C provides illustrative data on the sources of the various elements required for plant realization in a selected group of projects. In general, the information presented confirms the extent to which procurement and engineering services are undertaken by entities in the same country. One interesting exception is the case of Venoco in Venezuela, in which 48 percent of the equipment was produced locally although the basic and detailed engineering were carried out abroad. It is probable that local procurement was high in this case because the main source of financing was a government agency, and because the process involved (manufacturing dodecylbenzene) is relatively simple.

Even when the project owner himself nominally controls procurement, lack of experience may lead him to seek the advice of a contractor. The experience of Pemex, however, shows that direct procurement by a knowledgeable entity in a recipient country can cut costs significantly.

Pemex has procurement officers in Paris, London, and the United States, and has buyers' credits with French, American, and British banks. Through direct procurement, Pemex estimates that it has been able to reduce the price of purchased equipment by up to 40 percent.

To sum up, although dependence on foreign financing may be relatively low, a proportion of equipment has to be imported even into relatively advanced economies, such as those of Brazil and Mexico. The level of imports is partly a function of Latin American countries' continued dependence on foreign firms for basic engineering; partly a consequence of the lack of sophistication in recipients' capital goods sectors; and partly a function of their relatively small markets for such goods, which means they cannot reap the benefits of specialization based on economies of scale in capital goods production.

Local Project Management and Detailed Engineering

A distinction was drawn in chapter 1 between operational technology (the ability to run a completed plant) and project management and design technology (the ability to organize and implement a project from its initial conception through start-up, including the capacity to undertake the detailed and basic design engineering required to adapt an existing process, or design a new one, to meet the needs of a recipient). Although much of the knowledge for operational technology is transferred, project management and design capabilities are usually supplied by the technology owner (or his agent) and are not transferred to the recipient, in the sense that the latter is given little or no opportunity to master them for his own future use. This subsection briefly examines the extent to which Latin American countries have in fact developed indigenous capabilities for project management and detailed engineering.

PROJECT MANAGEMENT. The tasks involved in project management are complex and time consuming, and require a relatively high degree of technical expertise on the part of the manager in the recipient entity. It may be too costly (and risky) for a small firm with a single project to undertake all aspects of project management itself. A larger organization that may be involved in a succession of projects is in a quite different position, however; both internal and external benefits can be expected from the development of a project management capability. Expertise derived from learning-by-doing on one project can be applied to subsequent ones (internal); management's bargaining power with technology suppliers will be strengthened (internal); utilization of local engineering services and equipment suppliers will increase the expertise of these groups (external); and the greater use of local resources, both human and physical, brings the benefits (internal and external) of skill development, local income multiplier effects, and reduced foreign exchange expenditure.

Project management technology has reached a relatively high degree of sophistication in a few petrochemical organizations in Latin America, but key elements of management and organization are usually provided by the contractor who supplies the transfer package. The chief exceptions to this rule are Pemex in Mexico, Petroquisa in Brazil, and (at least initially) IVP in Venezuela. In addition, a few private engineering firms, such as Bufete Industrial in Mexico (see next subsection), have developed a degree of capability in this area.

The cases of Pemex and IVP are of special interest. Pemex developed its project management capability out of necessity. In its early years, it was subjected to an organized boycott by the large multinational firms which together nearly monopolized oil refining.[14] Many suppliers refused to sell equipment and materials to Pemex, which therefore found it necessary to develop the capacity to unpackage the technology it had already acquired and to organize and manage new projects itself. Pemex now contracts to the Instituto Mexicano de Petróleos (see next subsection) and other local engineering firms for detailed engineering, supervision and inspection of procurement, tender preparation, and other services.

In Venezuela, IVP has taken a different route. The technology for its first petrochemical plants, built between 1956 and 1962, was acquired with the maximum degree of unpackaging then possible.[15] In every case, IVP acquired the license for the process and the design of the plant from foreign firms, but IVP's own technical personnel undertook all other activities, using the advice of engineers provided by the process owners. IVP procured equipment directly through international bidding, and its staff carried out civil works, assembly and construction, and even start-up operations (though again with the help of foreign experts). Despite some inefficiency, IVP's direct involvement in every stage of the project gave it valuable project management experience which could have been utilized in later projects. After 1964, however, IVP decided to acquire petrochemical technology on a turnkey basis, so as to avoid the delays and extra costs that had occurred previously. As a result, the Venezuelan petrochemical industry had the worst of both worlds; it suffered the inevitable initial inefficiencies which are part of the price of learning by doing, but because IVP failed to maintain its commitment to developing indigenous expertise, the potential payoffs were lost for both IVP and local subcontractors.

Programs to develop local project management and technical capability are relatively rare even in state petrochemical enterprises in Latin America. In the absence of an explicit and consistently applied commitment to such policies at a national level, these enterprises tend to behave like private firms, opting for the short-term convenience of importing technology in a relatively packaged form. As the country-by-country information in the remainder of this chapter illustrates, the situation is similar (with a few notable exceptions) for detailed and basic engineering skills.

DETAILED ENGINEERING. Detailed engineering includes all the engineering work not specific to the core process to be used in a plant. It includes soil engineering, work on foundations and structures, civil, electrical, and mechanical engineering, detailed equipment design, plant and equipment layout work, and industrial and systems engineering. The skills and organizational capabilities required become progressively more complex as an engineering firm's capacity develops—from civil engineering through structural, mechanical, and electrical engineering to chemical plant engineering.

Developing countries that have experienced rapid urbanization and have implemented import substitution policies have generally also developed some degree of local engineering capacity. The engineering groups involved in detailed engineering for chemical and petrochemical plants in Mexico, Brazil, and Argentina (the Latin American countries with the most advanced detailed engineering capabilities) often started as civil engineering firms. In the Andean countries, civil engineering, soil engineering, electrical engineering, and other auxiliary engineering services are often carried out locally.

Local detailed engineering services may be incorporated even into a turnkey contract; the lower cost of engineering services generally in the recipient country provides an incentive for the contractor to obtain these services locally.[16] Some examples of the use of local firms for engineering services of various kinds are given in appendix C. The data show that, although civil and electrical engineering are fairly regularly subcontracted to local firms, detailed chemical engineering tends to be in the hands of the supplier of the core technology or another firm from the supplier's country.[17]

Argentina developed the capability to carry out detailed engineering for chemical and petrochemical projects in the 1950s within the (usually foreign-owned) large chemical firms, which created their own engineering departments, staffed with local engineers.[18] Local subsidiaries of foreign engineering firms also undertake detailed engineering. An example in Argentina is Fish International, a subsidiary of Fish Engineering and Construction, which has carried out the detailed engineering of six projects (all for Petroquímica Argentina S.A., in which Fish International has a 15 percent shareholding).

In Mexico, engineering firms able to carry out the detailed engineering of chemical and petrochemical plants have evolved independently of producers and have achieved a higher level of development than in Argentina. Although the first local engineering firm was founded in 1949, Pemex relied exclusively on international engineering firms until 1958, when it invited local engineering firms to collaborate in coordinating and supervising various project activities. Two years later, Bufete Industrial, a local firm, was doing the engineering work for a Pemex cyclohexane plant.

Pemex did not support the development of local engineering groups in its early years because of the risks associated with using inexperienced firms and the consequent potential threat to the supply of oil and its by-products to local markets. Pemex's attitude changed as local engineering firms gained experience by working with multinational contractors and as its own technical competence increased. In 1965, the state-owned Instituto Mexicano de Petróleos (IMP) was created to provide Pemex with technological services to maximize the efficiency of its existing plants and to execute new projects.[19]

More than twenty domestic engineering firms currently operate in Mexico. Of fourteen firms registered with the National Association of Engineering Firms by 1975, ten were wholly locally owned. Two had between 40 and 50 percent foreign shareholding and only two were wholly foreign-owned. By 1976, Bufete Industrial, the largest locally owned firm, had 10,000 employees including 1,500 professionals and technicians and had participated in the detailed engineering of fifty-two plants. Bufete participates in two-thirds of all Mexico's process industry projects, although there are a number of other fairly large local engineering firms.[20]

Foreign engineering firms, even those with associated firms in Mexico, sometimes enter directly into joint ventures or special arrangements with large local engineering groups. In these projects, the foreign firm usually carries out the basic engineering and the local firm undertakes detailed engineering and construction work. Thus, although most core technologies and basic engineering services are still imported, local firms have been able to provide 90 percent of all detailed engineering work undertaken in Mexico during the past decade.

As noted earlier, Pemex did not initially set out to foster local detailed engineering capabilities. In fact, local engineering firms were first used for detailed studies by foreign contractors rather than by Pemex. This was partly because of personal links between Bufete and one of the large international contractors, and partly because these contractors found it relatively cheap to use local engineers (and were presumably more willing to risk using local staff than Pemex was in its early years). Nevertheless, the present level of engineering capability in Mexico is largely attributable to Pemex's post-1958 policies. Such policies would have been too risky for a small local producer, which would have seen the development of local engineering capability as an externality. Over the years, however, Pemex and the Mexican petrochemical industry in general have come to save by using local engineering firms—and Mexican engineering groups are now even exporting their services.[21]

In Brazil, as in Mexico, foreign contractors find it profitable to use local firms to carry out detailed engineering because of the low cost of local engineering man-hours. Like Pemex—but more recently and somewhat less consistently—Petroquisa has favored the use of local firms for the detailed engineering of plants in which it participates. In Brazil, as in Mexico, the foreign contractor or licensor usually carries out the basic engineering and then subcontracts detailed engineering either to its own local subsidiary or to an independent local firm. Local firms carried out about 40 percent of the engineering of the plants which make up the Bahia petrochemical center. Again, as in Mexico, the local supply of engineering services is highly concentrated. In the Bahia complex, for example, the engineering for nine projects was undertaken by only three engineering firms, the largest in Brazil (Montreal Engenharia, Promon Engenharia, and Natron).[22] Each of these firms has a well-staffed technical department, employing between 300 and 500 engineers and technicians; all three have collaborated with international contractors in the engineering of local plants.

The establishment of local subsidiaries of multinational engineering firms is sometimes believed to be the most effective way of transferring engineering skills to developing countries. Another frequently discussed option is the creation of joint ventures between multinational engineering firms and local private or public entities. Brazil's experience with these arrangements seems to have been beneficial, because most of the personnel working in local subsidiaries or joint ventures are Brazilian nationals, and the skills they acquire are therefore likely to remain in the country. Where a subsidiary is competing with a locally owned engineering firm for the supply of the same services, however, the subsidiary is often in a relatively advantageous position—sometimes because of genuine technological superiority, but as often as not because of its financial or other links with the core technology supplier.[23] As a result, detailed engineering undertaken by local firms is often restricted to peripheral works.[24] As the examples in appendix C show, detailed engineering associated with the core plant is carried out mainly by the subsidiaries of foreign firms. Locally owned firms in Mexico seem to compete on better terms than their Brazilian counterparts—perhaps because Pemex has become more willing to assume the risks entailed by local firms' learning by doing, while Petroquisa's policies are more strongly influenced by calculations based on private costs and benefits.

With the exception of Chile, the Andean countries are very far behind Mexico, Brazil, and Argentina in their detailed engineering capabilities. For example, in Venezuela the engineering capacity of local firms is confined to civil works, electrical engineering, construction, and plant assembly. In Peru the participation of local consulting groups is generally limited to civil, sanitary, and electrical engineering works, although some firms have participated in activities such as materials handling or supervision of construction and assembly.[25] In every recent project promoted by Induperú, foreign firms performed all detailed as well as basic engineering for the plants. Chile's relatively advanced detailed engineering capabilities stem from the role played by Empresa Nacional de Petróleo (ENAP) in oil refining. As early as 1953, engineers from ENAP were able to design a solvent plant for a refinery in Chile. The participation of ENAP's process engineering division has grown steadily over the years; in certain cases, such as the construction in 1972–73 of a new plant for the same refinery, foreign technology imports have been limited to basic engineering only. In the case of small projects such as for the treatment and purification of oil products, ENAP engineers have been able to design plants, using process information given in license agreements.[26]

Basic Engineering and Process Development

Very few local entities in Latin America are able to carry out the basic engineering of petrochemical plants, which involves adapting the basic principles of a process to the specific conditions of a plant. This capability is a precondition for mastering the acquired technology and eventually generating new products or processes, but it has essentially been developed only in Mexico and, to a lesser extent, Brazil and Argentina.

In Mexico, IMP has developed some capacity for basic engineering as a result of its research and development activities, which concentrate on solving concrete problems for Pemex rather than on pure research. These activities have required IMP to master the engineering of processes already in use at Pemex plants. IMP's technical capacity has grown over time to the point where it has been able to offer its own technology, including four refining processes and six petrochemical processes. IMP has even exported technology, setting up two Pemex plants in the United States in 1974, and has signed agreements with U.S. firms for joint development and commercialization of process technologies.[27]

Imported petrochemical technology has on occasion been adapted to the needs of the relatively small Mexican market. Adaptations have been made possible by the availability of local research and development expertise and by Mexican engineers' access to laboratory data on processes examined but not used in developed countries.[28]

Local private engineering firms in Mexico have acquired only very limited basic engineering skills. This is partly because of the lack of advanced scientific and technological infrastructure (or research and development work other than that carried out by IMP) and partly because of the conditions sought by the licensors of technology, who usually provide process guarantees only if basic engineering is undertaken by a firm with international experience. Whenever possible, Pemex now negotiates the participation of Mexican engineers in basic engineering work on plants being built by foreign firms, in order to develop local expertise.[29] Participation with international engineering firms is either for a long-term joint venture or for the duration of a single project only. Long-term joint ventures may fail to maximize local engineers' opportunities for learning by doing, because the foreign partner may retain control of basic engineering and associated skills, leaving local firms to undertake detailed engineering only. Short-term associations for technical assistance in specific areas are often preferable, especially when the recipient has its own research and development capacity which permits it (as in the case of IMP) to assimilate the skills provided by the foreign firm.[30]

In Brazil the acquisition of local basic engineering and process development capability has also been closely linked to the technical needs of the country's state oil-refining enterprise, Petrobras. By the early 1960s, Petrobras staff could undertake all the studies required for oil refinery expansion; since 1962, foreign enterprises have been required to work with Brazilian firms when submitting tenders involving basic design work.

The research activities of Petrobras are undertaken by CENPES, an entity created in 1966 to provide technical assistance to Petrobras's operational activities. It has since expanded the scope of its work to cover research on improvements in petrochemical production processes, including the adaptation of existing processes and products to local conditions and raw materials. CENPES's activities have not, however, been sufficiently directed toward industrial applications of the results of its research. This state of affairs has held back the development of Petrobras's own process design capability. The situation has been exacerbated by delays in the creation of an engineering counterpart to CENPES.[31] Brazil consequently has little or no experience in basic design, process development, and pilot plant work.[32]

In Argentina a degree of basic engineering capability has been developed by local petrochemical producer firms. This has mainly taken the form, however, of adaptations or improvements of existing processes or the redesign of particular operations, rather than the basic engineering or design of complete processes. Given the structure of participation in Argentina's petrochemical industry, the majority of firms involved in process development are likely to be subsidiaries of foreign companies.

On the basis of the evidence presented here, it appears that the capability for basic engineering and project design is most likely to be developed by state-owned enterprises the size of IMP, Pemex, or Petroquisa, because only such enterprises have the needed resources or capacity for long-term planning. Even in large state enterprises such as these, however, operational and research activities and objectives may not be adequately articulated or integrated. As already noted, those in charge of day-to-day operations are liable to view the purchase of foreign technology as the most risk-free and effective way to start or expand production. Meanwhile, research and development groups, unable to influence the operational decisionmakers' technology choices, may tend to limit their work to research which is relatively remote from current industrial applications (as appears to have been the case with CENPES). Thus, in the absence of a clear strategy for the development of basic engineering skills at a national policymaking level, the mere existence of state enterprises does not in itself guarantee the acquisition of such skills.

Summary and Conclusion

This overview of local technological capabilities in Latin America has shown that the countries with the largest number of plants and the most active state enterprises (Mexico and Brazil) have the most extensive experience in the activities required for project realization. But even these countries have only a limited capacity for the basic engineering and project design work that represents a sine qua non for an independent, indigenous petrochemical industry. The acquisition of this capability (and of less sophisticated capabilities in other countries in the region) is inhibited by the scale and organization of the industry in recipient countries. Even if these problems could be overcome, however, recipients would still have to take account of the fact that technology is transferred under terms and conditions which may confine it to operational technology only and limit opportunities for local learning by doing. Thus, the contractual arrangements used in transfers may affect the broader process of technological development as a whole. What determines the form these arrangements take? This question is addressed in chapter 4, which presents an overview of some of the main factors that shape the nature of contracts for the transfer of petrochemical technology to Latin America.

Notes

1. Venezuela has had extraordinary start-up problems with the Tablazo complex north of Lake Maracaibo and operating problems at the Morón complex. By the beginning of 1979 the combined losses in both complexes had reached $800 million, and a complete reorganization of the projects was ordered under the authority of the government oil enterprise. The reorganization involved additional investment of more than $500 million and technical assistance contracts with Phillips Petroleum and Snam Progetti (*Chemical Week*, May 23, 1979, p. 28).

2. "Contracts shall not be approved when they refer to technology freely available in the country; when the price or counter-service is out of proportion to the technology acquired or constitutes an unwarranted or excessive burden on the country's economy; when they restrict the research or technological development of the purchaser; when they permit the technology supplier to interfere in the management of the purchaser company or enable it to use, on a permanent basis, the personnel appointed by the supplier; when they establish the obligation to purchase inputs from the supplier only or to sell the goods produced by the technology importer exclusively to the supplier company; when they prohibit or restrict the export of goods in a way contrary to the country's interest; when they limit the size of production or impose prices on domestic production or on exports by the purchaser; when they prohibit the use of complementary technology; when they oblige the importer to sign exclusive sales or representation contracts with the supplier company covering the national territory; when they establish excessively long terms of enforcement, which in no case may exceed a ten-year obligation on the importer company; or when they provide that claims arising from the interpretation or fulfillment of such contracts are to be submitted to the jurisdiction of foreign courts." Government of Mexico, *Law on the Transfer of Technology and the Use and Exploitation of Patents and Trademarks*.

3. J. Tavares de Araujo and Vera Maria Dick, "The Government, Multinational Enterprises and National Enterprises: The Case of the Brazilian Petrochemical Industry," *Pesquisa e Planejamento Econômico*, vol. 4, no. 3 (December 1974).

4. N. Mosso, E. Amadeo, and R. Fernandez, "La Industria Petroquímica Argentina" (Buenos Aires: Consejo Latinoamericano de Ciencias Sociales, 1976, processed).

5. T. S. Goho, "The Petrochemical Industry," in Jeve Behrman, *The Role of International Companies in Latin American Integration: Autos and Petrochemicals* (Lexington, Mass.: D. C. Heath, 1972).

6. Ibid.

7. The difficulties faced by Colombia's Monómeros Colombo Venezolanos S.A. in setting up a caprolactam plant illustrate the problems caused by the lack of local consulting capability. Prefeasibility and feasibility studies for the project were contracted to a foreign

firm which estimated the 1966 demand for caprolactam in Latin America at 13,700 metric tons a year. The project was finished in 1972 at a cost 50 percent higher than the original estimate. Moreover, demand in 1974 proved to be 30 percent lower than projected for that year, and export opportunities were even lower. Production costs were 300 percent above estimate, and the supply of raw materials was insufficient for the plant's needs. A local firm with greater knowledge of local conditions might have based its studies on more realistic assumptions. (See A. Gomez Prada, "Instalación de una Planta de Caprolactama en Colombia," paper presented at a working meeting of the chemical and petrochemical sector sponsored by the Organization of American States, Quito, April 1975.)

8. Economic Commission for Latin America (ECLA), *The Manufacture of Industrial Machinery and Equipment in Latin America*, vol. 1, *Basic Equipment in Brazil* (New York: United Nations, 1963).

9. When the initial plans for the expansion of this refinery were made by the foreign technology supplier, Kellogg, no provision was made for the use of Brazilian equipment. Because it proved difficult to obtain even medium-term credit from U.S. equipment manufacturers and because Petrobras had a substantial supply of cruzeiros at its disposal, it was decided to place certain orders in Brazil. In 1955, a group of Brazilian industrialists had founded the Brazilian Association for the Development of Basic Industry, whose objectives were (a) to study the specifications stipulated by Kellogg and adapt them (in close collaboration with the company's engineers) to the capability of the Brazilian metalworking industry, and (b) to give domestic producers technical advice to help them meet these specifications.

10. A. del Castillo, "Demandas de Equipo para las Plantas de Petróleos Mexicanos," Memoria del Primer Congreso de la Asociación Nacional de Firmas de Ingeniería, Mexico City, 1971.

11. A. Nadal, "La Política Tecnológica de la Empresa Estatal Petróleos Mexicanos" (Mexico City: Colegio de México, 1976; processed).

12. N. Mosso, E. Amadeo, and R. Fernández, "La Industria Petroquímica Argentina" (Buenos Aires: Consejo Latinoamericano de Ciencias Sociales, 1976; processed).

13. Ecosipro Ltd., "Investigación sobre la Política de Compras de Bienes de Capital en los Sectores Petroquímico y Siderúrgico," Caracas, June 1976. Processed.

14. M. Kamenetzky, "Process Engineering and Process Industries in Argentina and Mexico," study sponsored by the International Development Research Center of Canada (Buenos Aires, 1976; processed).

15. L. Reni, "La Transferencia de Tecnología en la Industria Petroquímica Básica Nacional" (Caracas: Centro de Estudios de la Administración Pública, Universidad Central de Venezuela, July 1975; processed).

16. A urea and ammonia complex owned by the Venezuelan government (90 percent) and the Colombian government (10 percent) is one example of the use of local engineering and construction firms within a turnkey arrangement. In this case, however, the supposed benefits of local subcontracting did not materialize. Because of the large number of intermediaries between the general contractors and the Venezuelan subcontractors, the latter received only about one-third of the total fee charged to the client for their services. Moreover, no equipment was purchased in Venezuela; equipment items were procured wholly (and without bidding) in six European countries which had provided credit for their purchase. Engineers in IVP have estimated that the consequent overpricing was around $20 million (the original contract was for $92 million).

17. The case of Estiluzia in Venezuela is of special interest because the original lump-sum contract agreed with the foreign contractor was renegotiated. In the event, only plant design and foreign procurement were undertaken by the contractor (Ortloff) on a cost plus basis; the remaining engineering services were subcontracted to local firms at reported savings of about 50 percent. (See M. A. Villanueva, "Comportamiento Tecnológico de las

Empresas Mixtas en la Industria Petroquímica," [Caracas: National Council for Scientific and Technical Research, June 1976; processed].)

18. One such group, which became an independent firm in 1975, carried out detailed engineering of over forty chemical processes within its first five years. Another firm, an affiliate of a transnational corporation, started operations in 1957; by the late 1970s, it had a professional staff of 220 in addition to 2,030 administrative personnel, clerks, and workers, and had participated in the detailed engineering of thirty-six chemical processes.

19. Some basic statistics offer an idea of the scale of IMP's operations. It has a payroll of 2,000 employees, 600 of which are professionals. It acts simultaneously as an engineering group designing industrial installations (mainly for Pemex), as a consultancy team organizing petroleum and petrochemical investment projects, and as a technological institute developing processes for the chemical and petrochemical subsectors. By 1974, the project engineering department of IMP had completed eleven projects for Pemex costing over $63 million. Projects in the pipeline involved an investment value at least six times this figure. The fees paid by Pemex to IMP in 1970 were 30 percent lower than the sums it would have had to pay foreign engineering firms for the same services. By 1974, one hour of IMP's engineering work cost $12, about half the rate charged by foreign engineering firms. The services of IMP and other local engineering firms thus represent a considerable foreign exchange saving for Mexico. (See A. de La Vega Navarro, "La Société Nationale Mexicaine Pemex et l'Engineering," Institut de Recherche Economique et Planification, Université des Sciences Sociales de Grenoble, December 1970.)

20. A. Nadal, "Engineering Firms in Mexico" (Mexico City: Colegio de México, May 1976; processed).

21. Tecnimexico S.A. de C.V. is an association made up of 29 engineering firms. With backing from the Mexican government these firms have contributed to exports of services to Barbados, Belize, Bolivia, Brazil, Canada, Colombia, the Dominican Republic, Ecuador, El Salvador, Guatemala, Honduras, Panama, Peru, and Venezuela. (See A. Nadal, "Engineering Firms in Mexico.")

22. J. Tavares de Araujo and Vera Maria Dick, "The Government, Multinational Enterprises and National Enterprises."

23. Sergio F. Alves and Ecila M. Ford, "O Comportamento das Empresas Estatais: A Selecão das Empresas de Engineering, a Escolha de Processos Industriais e a Compra de Bens de Capital," study prepared by the Grupo de Pesquisas, Financiadora Nacional de Estudos e Projetos, São Paulo, June 1975.

24. Tavares and Dick, "The Government, Multinational Enterprises and National Enterprises."

25. Science and Technology Policy Instruments Study, Peruvian Group, "La Situación de la Actividad de Ingeniería en el Perú," sponsored by the International Development Research Center of Canada (Lima: Oficina Nacional de Planificación, Lima, October 1975; processed).

26. Gonzales J. Yanez, "La Ingeniería de Procesos en la Empresa Nacional del Petróleo," *Revista de la Empresa Nacional del Petróleo* (Santiago, 1975).

27. A. Nadal, "La Política Tecnológica de la Empresa Estatal Petróleos Mexicanos."

28. José B. Giral and R. P. Morgan, "Appropriate Technology for Chemical Industries in Developing Countries," a report prepared in connection with Foreign Area Fellowship Programme held at National Autonomous University of Mexico, Mexico City, July–August 1972.

29. A. Nadal, "Engineering Firms in Mexico."

30. A. de La Vega Navarro and J. Perrin, "Desarrollo y Fortalecimiento de la Ingeniería en México" (Mexico City: Colegio de México, December 1974; processed).

31. A study carried out in the mid-1970s recommended the creation of a basic engineer-

ing group linked to Petroquisa, following the example of Ente Nazionale de Idrocarburi (ENI) and Snam Progetti in Italy or IMP and Pemex in Mexico (see Alves and Ford, "O Comportamento das Empresas Estatais"). It was suggested that this would encourage linkages between petrochemical engineering work and production activities. Other expected advantages included better absorption and adaptation of technologies acquired from abroad, and higher levels of participation in the petrochemical industry on the part of local private engineering firms and equipment producers.

32. K. Politzer, "Projeto de Processamento," paper presented at the Simposium Semana de Tecnologia Industrial, sponsored by Ministerio de Indústria y Comércio, São Paulo, September 1975.

Chapter 4

Summary and Synthesis

Previous chapters have suggested some of the issues involved when technology suppliers and recipients negotiate and agree on the terms and conditions for transfers of petrochemical technology to Latin America. This chapter begins with a summary outline of these issues. It then presents a synthesis, based on empirical data collected for 280 different plants, of the relative importance of four key variables in determining the kinds of arrangements for transfer agreed to by technology suppliers and recipients.

The Issues

Chapter 1 presented some elements of the conceptual framework underlying discussions of technology transfers. In particular, it described the concept of unpackaged versus packaged transfers of technology, noted some of the questions raised by academics and policymakers about the effects of packaged transfers on indigenous technological development, and suggested that there might nevertheless be practical reasons for both suppliers and recipients of technology to feel that relatively packaged transfers were in their private interests. The different motives of producer and nonproducer suppliers of technology were discussed, as well as the terms and conditions for transfer which they might favor. Questions were raised about externalities and the social and private costs and benefits of packaged transfer arrangements. The two main so-called neotechnology theories of technology transfer were briefly described: the technology gap theory and the product life-cycle theory. Both emphasize the influence of the maturity of the product on the types of transfer arrangements used. It was suggested that the theories might be of limited application to petrochemical technology transfers between developed and developing countries—in particular because of industry characteristics such as the specialization of technology ownership by product type, the frequency of process innovation in the industry, and the relative unimportance of labor costs in petrochemical projects.

Chapter 2 dealt with the suppliers of petrochemical technology to Latin America. Using concrete examples and statistical data, the text demonstrated empirically some of the broad tendencies described in more general and abstract terms in chapter 1. Among other things it showed that there was strong evidence for a marked bifurcation of ownership of processes by type of owner and product group, with producers owning virtually all processes for the manufacture of final products and nonproducers predominating in the ownership of processes for making basic products. This pattern of specialization applied in transfers of technology for final and basic products as well as in process ownership. Transfers of technology for intermediate products have in the past been divided almost evenly between the two supplier groups, but the trend in recent years has been toward more transfers by nonproducers in this subsector.

The relatively large number of potential suppliers of most processes, together with technical factors in the industry such as the potential for process innovation regardless of product maturity, the development of close substitutes, and the relatively similar technical capability of major suppliers have favored a competitive market for petrochemical processes. Competition has been reduced, however, by institutional and technical factors such as the formal and informal links between different participants on the supply side of the market, and the fact that different processes require different inputs and produce different by-products.

Suppliers' bargaining strength in relation to recipients and their ability to negotiate packaged transfers have been enhanced by the high degree of sophistication of engineering contractors, equipment fabricators, financing agencies, and the like in developed countries, as compared with their counterparts in recipients' countries. The two supplier groups differed in their attitude toward contractual arrangements for transfers, with nonproducers limiting their participation to pre-start-up activities and producers tending to favor contractual arrangements which gave them some degree of participation (financial or operational) in recipients' post-start-up activities. Individual contracts (and therefore degrees of participation) varied widely, however, depending on factors such as supplier size and product orientation, and the characteristics of recipient country markets.

Chapter 3 examined the recipients of petrochemical technology in Latin America. Again using examples and data collected for this study, together with information in the existing literature, it described the structure of capacity in the Latin American petrochemical industry by country (in terms of existing or planned output volume and number of plants) and suggested that country and market factors might affect the particular type of contractual arrangement used for transfers of technology. The structure of participation in the industry was examined, with emphases on the regulatory framework governing transfers in different countries and the relative importance of different types of participant (local public enterprises, local private enterprises, and foreign firms). Also analyzed were the differences in levels of indigenous technological capacity among countries and some of the factors contributing to these variations.

Determinants of Contractual Arrangements

In general, the discussion in earlier chapters has distinguished between contractual arrangements which are relatively liberal (involving straight license agreements) or relatively restrictive (providing for supplier participation in recipients' post-start-up operations). The likelihood that a particular contract will be of one type or the other has been linked to four broad groups of factors: the type of product for which technology is transferred; the maturity of the product to be manufactured and of the process to be used; the nature of the recipient of the technology; and the nature of the supplier of the technology. Evidence from the survey of 280 plants shows the relationships between each of these groups of factors and contractual arrangements involving straight licensing on the one hand and varying degrees of supplier participation in ownership of the recipient entity on the other.

The term "straight license agreement" may cover a multitude of real-life situations. These range from a completely unrestricted license for the recipient to use the technology transferred in whatever way he wishes, to provisions which may profoundly affect the recipient's post-start-up activities even if the supplier takes no shares in the recipient entity. Thus, it cannot be assumed that recipients who are classified as obtaining technology under straight license agreements are necessarily free to go their own way after start-up without being subject to any supplier influence. Further, straight license agreements can involve very highly packaged transfers of pre-start-up technology. In our sample, half the contracts of this type whose details we were able to establish had the licensor also supplying engineering and contracting services (see table 2-8).

In some cases a contractual arrangement will be described below as a straight license agreement, but the supplier may have majority or even total ownership of the recipient. These cases arise when a producer company sets up a wholly owned or majority-owned subsidiary in a developing country, but obtains the technology for it from a nonproducer (or another producer) under a straight license agreement.

As table 4-1 shows, a significant proportion of agreements defined as straight license agreements (SLAs) in fact involves either total or majority

Table 4-1. *Relationship between Type of Technology Agreement and Degree of Local and Foreign Ownership: 280 Petrochemical Plants*

Type of technology agreement	(a) Locally owned		(b) Foreign minority		(c) Local control (a) + (b)		(d) Equal shares		(e) Foreign majority	
	Number	Percent	Number	Percent	Number	Percent	Number	Percent	Number	Percent
1 Local technology	3	100	0	0	3	100	0	0	0	0
2 Straight license	98	66	23	16	121	82	1	1	10	7
3 Minority participation	0	0	32	86	32	86	0	0	4	11
4 Subtotal (1 + 2 + 3)	101	54	55	29	156	83	1	1	14	7
5 Shared participation	0	0	0	0	0	0	2	100	0	0
6 Majority participation	0	0	0	0	0	0	0	0	11	92
7 Subsidiary	0	0	0	0	0	0	0	0	0	0
8 Subtotal (6 + 7)	0	0	0	0	0	0	0	0	11	26
9 All known (4 + 5 + 8)	101	44	55	24	156	68	3	1	25	11
10 Participation, but extent unknown	0	0	0	0	0	0	0	0	0	0
11 Not known whether any participation	24	65	2	5	26	70	1	3	2	5
12 Total (9 + 10 + 11)	125	47	57	21	182	68	4	1	27	10

Type of technology agreement	(f) Subsidiary		(g) Foreign control (e)+(f)		(h) All known (c)+(d)+(g)		(i) Foreign percentage unknown	(j) Owner-ship not known	(k) Total number (h)+(i)+(j)
	Number	Percent	Number	Percent	Number	Percent			
1 Local technology	0	0	0	0	3	100	0	0	3
2 Straight license	15	10	25	17	147	100	0	1	148
3 Minority participation	1	3	5	14	37	100	0	0	37
4 Subtotal (1 + 2 + 3)	16	9	30	16	187	100	0	1	188
5 Shared participation	0	0	0	0	2	100	0	0	2
6 Majority participation	1	8	12	100	12	100	0	0	12
7 Subsidiary	30	100	30	100	30	100	0	0	30
8 Subtotal (6 + 7)	31	74	42	100	42	100	0	0	42
9 All known (4 + 5 + 8)	47	20	72	31	231	100	0	1	232
10 Participation, but extent unknown	0	0	0	0	0	0	3	0	3
11 Not known whether any participation	8	22	10	27	37	100	4	4	45
12 Total (9 + 10 + 11)	55	21	82	31	268	100	7	5	280

Note: All percentages are proportions of row subtotals in column (h); items may not add to totals because of rounding.

113

Table 4-2. Relationship between Type of Product and Type of Technology Agreement: 280 Petrochemical Plants

Type of product	(a) Local technology		(b) Straight license (SLA)		(c) Minority participation		(d) Subtotal (a)+(b)+(c)		(e) Shared participation	
	Number	Per cent	Number	Per cent	Number	Per cent	Number	Per cent	Number	Per cent
Basic	0	0	64	94	2	3	66	97	0	0
Intermediate	2	2	71	70	15	15	88	87	0	0
Final	1	2	13	21	20	32	34	54	2	3
Total	3	1	148	64	37	16	188	81	2	1

Type of product	(f) Majority participation		(g) Subsidiary		(h) Licensor control (f)+(g)		(i) All known (d)+(e)+(h)		(j) Participation, but extent unknown	(k) Participation not known	(l) Total number (i)+(j)+(k)
	Number	Per cent	Number	Per cent	Number	Per cent	Number	Per cent			
Basic	0	0	2	3	2	3	68	100	0	9	77
Intermediate	5	5	8	8	13	13	101	100	1	18	120
Final	7	11	20	32	27	43	63	100	2	18	83
Total	12	5	30	13	42	18	232	100	3	45	280

Note: All percentages are proportions of row subtotals in column (i); items may not add to 100 percent because of rounding.

foreign ownership of the recipient entity. No less than 25 of the 147 SLAS for plants whose ownership was known involved transfers to plants which were wholly or mainly foreign-owned (17 percent of all such agreements). Put the other way round, the technology for 15 of the 47 entities in the sample categorized as subsidiaries, and 10 of the 25 categorized as majority foreign-owned, was obtained under straight license agreements (32 percent and 40 percent respectively of these subcategories).

It would thus be simplistic to assume that straight license agreements necessarily free the recipient from external influence, since the agreement may specify pre-start-up arrangements or post-start-up conditions that govern the way the licensee operates his plant and limit his freedom of action. Furthermore, as table 4-1 shows, the type of technology agreement is not necessarily congruent with the degree of foreign ownership. These points should be borne in mind in the discussions that follow.

Type of Product

Tables 4-2 and 4-3 provide data on the types of technology agreement used and the extent of foreign ownership found in the 280 plant sample, broken down by type of product. The incidence of local control, in terms of type of agreement and degree of ownership, appears to vary systematically with product type. Processes to manufacture basic products were overwhelmingly transferred under SLAS (94 percent), and the ownership of the plants producing them was predominantly local (62 percent sole ownership plus 16 percent minority foreign ownership, or 78 percent in all). The fact that the proportion of SLAS is noticeably higher than the proportion mainly or wholly locally owned reflects the imperfect congruence between transfer arrangements and ownership discussed above.

In the case of intermediate products, both SLAS and predominantly local ownership characterized about 70 percent of all transfers. Final products showed a very much lower proportion of SLAS (only 21 percent) and a significantly lower incidence of majority or total local ownership (53 percent in all).

The strong linkage between type of product and type of transfer agreement reflects the specialization of suppliers' ownership of different technology by product type (documented earlier in table 2-1) and their even stronger specialization in transfers by product type (table 2-2), together with their contrasting interests and contractual preferences with regard to transfers. The only surprise in tables 4-2 and 4-3 is the relatively small proportion of plants manufacturing final products which were subsidiaries or under majority foreign ownership—since producers, who are the sources of most technologies transferred for final products, are gener-

Table 4-3. *Relationship between Type of Product and Degree of Local and Foreign Ownership: 280 Petrochemical Plants*

	(a) Wholly local		(b) Foreign minority		(c) Local control (a)+(b)		(d) Shared ownership		(e) Foreign majority	
Type of product	Number	Per-cent	Number	Per-cent	Number	Per-cent	Number	Per-cent	Number	Per-cent
Basic	48	62	12	16	60	78	1	1	5	6
Intermediate	59	50	24	21	83	71	0	0	15	13
Final	18	24	21	28	39	53	3	4	7	9
Total	125	47	57	21	182	68	4	1	27	10

	(f) Subsidiary		(g) Foreign control (e)+(f)		(h) All known (c)+(d)+(g)		(i) Foreign owner-ship, but extent unknown	(j) Owner-ship not known	(k) Total number (h)+(i)+(j)
Type of product	Number	Per-cent	Number	Per-cent	Number	Per-cent			
Basic	11	14	16	21	77	100	0	0	77
Intermediate	19	16	34	29	117	100	1	2	120
Final	25	34	32	43	74	100	6	3	83
Total	55	21	82	31	268	100	7	5	280

Note: All percentages are proportions of row subtotals in column (h); items may not add to 100 percent because of rounding.

116

ally interested in taking a substantial ownership share in recipient entities. This situation probably reflects (a) recipient countries' regulations on ownership, which have increasingly discouraged foreign control of local companies—both in the petrochemical industry and more generally; (b) the relative flexibility that producers are willing to show in tailoring transfer arrangements to recipient country conditions; and (c) the fact that technology owners can in reality have quite a significant influence over recipient entities even when they do not have a majority shareholding in them.

Statistical tests of the data confirmed that the type of product was strongly linked to the type of contractual arrangement used.[1] The product life-cycle theory suggests, however, that the terms and conditions under which technology is transferred might vary systematically with product maturity. The next subsection uses survey data to examine the extent to which this is true in the case of contractual agreements for the transfer of petrochemical technology to Latin America.

Maturity of the Product and Process, and Age of Plant

Three measures are used to relate contractual arrangements to maturity factors. To use product maturity alone would be to ignore one of the main characteristics of the petrochemical industry—that process innovations can take place even after a product is fully matured. Table 4-4 therefore examines the incidence of different types of contractual arrangement in terms of product maturity, while table 4-5 conducts a parallel analysis on the basis of process maturity. The third criterion, period of plant construction (table 4-6), is used to check the extent to which contractual arrangements follow a pattern similar to that observed for sources of transfer, in which nonproducers have assumed increasing importance in more recent years.

The data in table 4-4 show types of licensing agreements for each product subgroup, broken down by the lag in years between the first commercialization of the product in the world and its first use in Latin America. If product maturity is a determinant of the type of transfer agreement used, the technology for products with the *longest* lag between first use in the world and in Latin America should be mainly transferred through SLAS, which are increasingly used as products become more standardized and mature. The proportion of transfers involving subsidiaries or majority foreign participation should rise as the lag time shortens, because in its early years a given technology remains in the hands of product innovators, who will wish to retain control over its use (see the discussion of the product life-cycle theory in chapter 1).

Table 4-4. *Relationship between Type of Technology Agreement and Maturity of Product: 280 Petrochemical Plants*

Maturity of product[a]	(a) Local technology		(b) Straight license (SLA)		(c) Minority participation		(d) Local control (a)+(b)+(c)		(e) Shared participation	
	Number	Percent	Number	Percent	Number	Percent	Number	Percent	Number	Percent
Basic products										
Over 40	0	0	41	91	2	4	43	95	0	0
30–39	0	0	17	100	0	0	17	100	0	0
20–29	0	0	5	100	0	0	5	100	0	0
Under 20	0	0	1	100	0	0	1	100	0	0
All known	0	0	64	94	2	3	66	97	0	0
Lag unknown	0	0	0	0	0	0	0	0	0	0
Total	0	0	64	94	2	3	66	97	0	0
Intermediate products										
Over 40	1	2	43	75	6	11	50	88	0	0
30–39	0	0	16	73	5	23	21	95	0	0
20–29	1	7	9	64	4	29	14	100	0	0
Under 20	0	0	0	0	0	0	0	0	0	0
All known	2	2	68	73	15	16	85	91	0	0
Lag unknown	0	0	3	38	0	0	3	38	0	0
Total	2	2	71	70	15	15	88	87	0	0
Final products										
Over 40	0	0	3	17	9	50	12	67	0	0
30–39	1	5	5	26	6	32	12	63	2	11
20–29	0	0	4	24	3	18	7	41	0	0
Under 20	0	0	1	50	1	50	2	100	0	0
All known	1	2	13	23	19	34	33	59	2	4
Lag unknown	0	0	0	0	1	14	1	14	0	0
Total	1	2	13	21	20	32	34	54	2	3

Maturity of product[a]	(f) Majority participation		(g) Subsidiary		(h) Licensor control (f)+(g)		(i) All known (d)+(e)+(h)		(j) Participation, but extent unknown	(k) Participation not known	(l) Total number (i)+(j)+(k)
	Number	Percent	Number	Percent	Number	Percent	Number	Percent			
Basic products											
Over 40	0	0	2	4	2	4	45	100	0	4	49
30–29	0	0	0	0	0	0	17	100	0	3	20
20–29	0	0	0	0	0	0	5	100	0	0	5
Under 20	0	0	0	0	0	0	1	100	0	0	1
All known	0	0	2	3	2	3	68	100	0	7	75
Lag unknown	0	0	0	0	0	0	0	0	0	2	2
Total	0	0	2	3	2	3	68	100	0	9	77
Intermediate products											
Over 40	3	5	4	7	7	12	57	100	1	13	71
30–39	1	5	0	0	1	5	22	100	0	2	24
20–29	0	0	0	0	0	0	14	100	0	0	14
Under 20	0	0	0	0	0	0	0	0	0	0	0
All known	4	4	4	4	8	9	93	100	1	15	109
Lag unknown	1	13	4	50	5	63	8	100	0	3	11
Total	5	5	8	8	13	13	101	100	1	18	120
Final products											
Over 40	2	11	4	22	6	33	18	100	0	2	20
30–39	3	16	2	11	5	26	19	100	1	2	22
20–29	2	12	8	47	10	59	17	100	0	7	24
Under 20	0	0	0	0	0	0	2	100	1	2	4
All known	7	13	14	25	21	38	56	100	1	13	70
Lag unknown	0	0	6	68	6	86	7	100	1	5	13
Total	7	11	20	32	27	43	63	100	2	18	83

Note: All percentages are proportions of row subtotals in column (i); items may not add to totals because of rounding.

a. Product maturity is measured by the lag in years between first production worldwide and first use of the technology in Latin America.

Table 4-5. *Relationship between Type of Technology Agreement and Maturity of Process: 280 Petrochemical Plants*

Maturity of process[a]	(a) Local technology		(b) Straight license (SLA)		(c) Minority participation		(d) Local control (a)+(b)+(c)		(e) Shared participation	
	Number	Percent	Number	Percent	Number	Percent	Number	Percent	Number	Percent
Basic products										
Over 20	0	0	11	92	1	8	12	100	0	0
15–19	0	0	4	100	0	0	4	100	0	0
10–14	0	0	16	100	0	0	16	100	0	0
5–9	0	0	13	100	0	0	13	100	0	0
Under 5	0	0	4	100	0	0	4	100	0	0
All known	0	0	48	98	1	2	49	100	0	0
Lag unknown	0	0	16	84	1	5	17	89	0	0
Total	0	0	64	94	2	3	66	97	0	0
Intermediate products										
Over 20	0	0	2	40	2	40	4	80	0	0
15–19	0	0	10	71	2	14	12	86	0	0
10–14	0	0	10	63	6	38	16	100	0	0
5–9	0	0	11	73	3	20	14	93	0	0
Under 5	1	8	10	77	0	0	11	85	0	0
All known	2	2	43	68	13	21	57	90	0	0
Lag unknown	1	3	28	74	2	5	31	82	0	0
Total	2	2	71	70	15	15	88	87	0	0
Final products										
Over 20	0	0	2	33	3	30	5	83	0	0
15–19	0	0	1	25	2	30	3	75	0	0
10–14	0	0	0	0	1	100	1	100	0	0
5–9	0	0	3	27	3	27	6	55	1	9
Under 5	1	33	0	0	0	0	1	33	0	0
All known	1	4	6	24	9	36	16	64	1	4
Lag unknown	0	0	7	18	11	29	18	47	1	3
Total	1	2	13	21	20	32	34	54	2	3

Maturity of process[a]	(f) Majority participation Number	Percent	(g) Subsidiary Number	Percent	(h) Licensor control (f)+(g) Number	Percent	(i) All known (d)+(e)+(h) Number	Percent	(j) Licensor participation, extent unknown	(k) Participation not known	(l) Total number (i)+ (j)+(k)
Basic products											
Over 20	0	0	0	0	0	0	12	100	0	0	12
15–19	0	0	0	0	0	0	4	100	0	0	4
10–14	0	0	0	0	0	0	16	100	0	0	16
5–9	0	0	0	0	0	0	13	100	0	0	13
Under 5	0	0	0	0	0	0	4	100	0	0	4
All known	0	0	0	0	0	0	49	100	0	0	49
Lag unknown	0	0	2	11	2	1	19	100	0	9	28
Total	0	0	2	3	2	3	68	100	0	9	77
Intermediate products											
Over 20	0	0	1	20	1	20	5	100	0	0	5
15–19	1	7	1	7	2	14	14	100	0	0	14
10–14	0	0	0	0	0	0	16	100	0	0	16
5–9	1	7	0	0	1	7	15	100	0	0	15
Under 5	1	8	1	8	2	15	13	100	0	0	13
All known	3	5	3	5	6	10	63	100	0	0	63
Lag unknown	2	5	5	13	7	18	38	100	1	18	57
Total	5	5	8	8	13	13	101	100	1	18	120
Final products											
Over 20	0	0	1	17	1	17	6	100	0	0	6
15–19	0	0	1	25	1	25	4	100	0	0	4
10–14	0	0	0	0	0	0	1	100	0	0	1
5–9	1	9	3	27	4	36	11	100	0	0	11
Under 5	0	0	2	67	2	67	3	100	0	0	3
All known	1	4	7	28	8	32	25	100	0	0	25
Lag unknown	6	16	13	34	19	50	38	100	2	18	58
Total	7	11	20	32	27	43	63	100	2	18	83

Note: All percentages are proportions of row subtotals in column (i); items may not add to totals because of rounding.
a. Maturity of process is measured by the lag in years between first commercialization worldwide and first use in Latin America.

Table 4-6. Relationship between Type of Technology Agreement and Age of Plant: 280 Petrochemical Plants

Age of plant[a]	(a) Local technology		(b) Straight license (SLA)		(c) Minority participation		(d) Local control (a)+(b)+(c)		(e) Shared participation	
	Number	Percent	Number	Percent	Number	Percent	Number	Percent	Number	Percent
Basic products										
Pre-1960	0	0	5	100	0	0	5	100	0	0
1960–69	0	0	26	90	2	7	28	97	0	0
Post-1969	0	0	33	97	0	0	33	97	0	0
All known	0	0	64	94	2	3	66	97	0	0
Date unknown	0	0	0	0	0	0	0	0	0	0
Total	0	0	64	94	2	3	66	97	0	0
Intermediate products										
Pre-1960	1	14	3	43	1	14	5	71	0	0
1960–69	1	3	31	82	2	5	34	89	0	0
Post-1969	0	0	34	71	12	25	46	96	0	0
All known	2	2	68	73	15	16	85	91	0	0
Date unknown	0	0	3	38	0	0	3	38	0	0
Total	2	2	71	70	15	15	88	87	0	0
Final products										
Pre-1960	0	0	1	14	0	0	1	14	0	0
1960–69	1	4	5	20	6	24	12	48	2	8
Post-1969	0	0	7	29	13	54	20	83	0	0
All known	1	2	13	23	19	34	33	59	2	4
Date unknown	0	0	0	0	1	14	1	14	0	0
Total	1	2	13	21	20	32	34	53	2	3

	(f) Majority participation		(g) Subsidiary		(h) Licensor control (f) + (g)		(i) All known (d) + (e) + (h)		(j) Licensor participation, extent unknown	(k) Participation not known	(l) Total number (i) + (j) + (k)
Age of plant[a]	Number	Percent	Number	Percent	Number	Percent	Number	Percent			
Basic products											
Pre-1960	0	0	0	0	0	0	5	100	0	1	6
1960–69	0	0	1	3	1	3	29	100	0	2	31
Post-1969	0	0	1	3	1	3	34	100	0	4	38
All known	0	0	2	3	2	3	68	100	0	7	75
Date unknown	0	0	0	0	0	0	0	0	0	2	2
Total	0	0	2	3	2	3	68	100	0	9	77
Intermediate products											
Pre-1960	2	29	0	0	2	29	7	100	0	1	8
1960–69	1	3	3	8	4	11	38	100	0	3	41
Post-1969	1	2	1	2	2	4	48	100	1	11	60
All known	4	4	4	4	8	9	93	100	1	15	109
Date unknown	1	13	4	50	5	63	8	100	0	3	11
Total	5	5	8	8	13	13	101	100	1	18	120
Final products											
Pre-1960	2	29	4	57	6	86	7	100	0	2	9
1960–69	3	12	8	32	11	44	25	100	1	1	27
Post-1969	2	8	2	8	4	17	24	100	0	10	34
All known	7	13	14	25	21	38	56	100	1	13	70
Date unknown	0	0	6	86	6	86	7	100	1	5	13
Total	7	11	20	32	27	43	63	100	2	18	83

Note: All percentages are proportions of row subtotals in column (i); items may not add to totals because of rounding.

a. Age of plant refers to period of construction.

In fact, as table 4-4 shows, basic products are transferred almost entirely through straight license agreements, regardless of the length of the lag. Intermediate products are also almost wholly transferred through SLAS regardless of the time lag—although there is some proportionate reduction in SLAS and some proportionate increase in minority foreign participation as the lag shortens. Only in the case of technologies for the manufacture of final products does the pattern show some resemblance to the kind of progression which might be expected if product maturity were a determinant of the type of agreement used for transfer. Ignoring the two newest plants (with a product commercialization lag of less than 20 years), there are proportionately more agreements involving local control and fewer involving subsidiaries of foreign firms in plants manufacturing mature products (those with a production lag of more than 40 years), and fewer involving licensing and more involving subsidiaries in the case of products with lags of 20 to 29 years.

Table 4-5 provides summary data on the links between type of contractual arrangement and the maturity of the processes used. Again, more mature processes (those first used in Latin America after a lag of 20 or more years since their first use worldwide) should be mainly transferred through SLAS, while those used after a shorter time lag should have higher proportions of foreign participation as the lag shortens. Again, the data resemble this pattern for final products only. For this subgroup, the proportion of agreements involving subsidiaries rises with the novelty of the process (that is, there are proportionately more agreements of this kind as the lag time in years shortens), while the trend is in the opposite direction for straight license agreements and agreements involving minority participations taken together (if the single observation in the 10–14 years cell is ignored, these agreements become more frequent the longer the lag in years).

When statistical tests were applied to tables 4-4 and 4-5, the results confirmed that the variations were significant only for final products. The patterns in table 4-5 for intermediate products appeared to be *contrary* to what might be expected if maturity determined the type of contractual arrangement used; on the basis of an admittedly small sample, the proportion of transfers involving subsidiaries *fell* with newer processes, that is, those with shorter time lags.

The types of contractual arrangements used were analyzed according to the age of the 280 plants surveyed (table 4-6). It appeared that the proportion of plants under local control rose with the recentness of plant construction in the case of both intermediate and final products—that is, plants that had been constructed or were planned to be constructed after

1970 were more likely to have had their technology transferred either through SLAS or through agreements specifying minority participation than ones built earlier. The data thus appear to indicate a reduction of supplier participation in more recent periods.

Table 4-7 confirms the tendency for technology to be transferred under relatively more liberal conditions in recent years. The table breaks down the sample of 127 plants whose technology was supplied by *producers* according to their period of construction. In the case of the earliest plants (those built before 1960), 29 percent of recipient entities were subsidiaries of suppliers; the latter had a minority interest in 7 percent of recipient entities and used SLAS to transfer technology in 29 percent of the cases. By contrast, the data for the latest plants (built since 1969) show subsidiaries as accounting for only 6 percent, minority participation rising to 51 percent, and SLAS also increasing to 36 percent. These findings are consistent with trends noted earlier, such as the increasing role of Latin American governments as regulators and of state enterprises as participants in the industry, rising levels of indigenous technical expertise in several countries, and an increasingly flexible supplier response to these trends.

On the basis of the data presented here, it does not appear that maturity of product, process, or plant is a significant determinant of the contractual arrangements used for petrochemical technology transfers to Latin America, except possibly with regard to final products. The analysis in this subsection has been by no means fruitless, however. Apart from showing the weakness of product/process maturity and age of plant as determinants of contractual arrangements, examination of the data has clearly illustrated the trend toward more liberal terms of transfer in recent years. This does not, however, mean that suppliers have necessarily relinquished their influence over recipients. Although the proportion of new plants under foreign control appears to be falling, the absolute number of new plants with some degree of foreign participation is rising, and, as noted in chapter 2, licensors can exert substantial influence over recipients even when they transfer technology through agreements involving only minority participation in ownership.

It was suggested above that the trend toward the use of more liberal contractual arrangements for transfers was in line with the more stringent regulations on foreign ownership introduced by recipient countries in recent years. This in turn implies that factors related to recipients' countries may represent an important determinant of the type of contractual arrangement used. Survey evidence on this point is presented in the next subsection.

Table 4-7. *Relationship between Type of Technology Agreement and Age of Plant When Technology Supplied by Producer: 127 Petrochemical Plants*

Age of plant[a]	(a) Local technology		(b) Straight license (SLA)		(c) Minority participation		(d) Local control (a)+(b)+(c)		(e) Shared participation	
	Number	Percent	Number	Percent	Number	Percent	Number	Percent	Number	Percent
Pre-1960	1	7	4	29	1	7	6	43	0	0
1960–69	2	4	19	39	10	20	31	63	2	4
Post-1969	0	0	17	36	24	51	41	87	0	0
All known	3	3	40	36	35	32	78	71	2	2
Date unknown	0	0	1	8	1	8	2	15	0	0
Total	3	2	41	33	36	29	80	65	2	2

Age of plant[a]	(f) Majority participation		(g) Subsidiary		(h) Licensor control (f)+(g)		(i) All known (d)+(e)+(h)		(j) Licensor participation, extent unknown	(k) Participation not known	(l) Total number (i)+(k)
	Number	Percent	Number	Percent	Number	Percent	Number	Percent			
Pre-1960	4	29	4	29	8	57	14	100	0	0	14
1960–69	4	8	12	24	16	33	49	100	1	0	50
Post-1969	3	6	3	6	6	13	47	100	1	1	49
All known	11	10	19	17	30	27	110	100	2	1	113
Date unknown	1	8	10	77	11	85	13	100	1	0	14
Total	12	10	29	24	41	33	123	100	3	1	127

Note: All percentages are proportions of row subtotals in column (i); items may not add to totals because of rounding.
a. Age of plant refers to period of construction.

Recipients' Country

The discussion in chapter 3 gave some impression of the scale of different countries' operations in the petrochemical industry, the regulatory systems in force (for both petrochemicals and foreign investment in general), the role played by state enterprises, and the varying degrees of indigenous technological development. It was noted that these factors would be likely to have a bearing on the overall pattern of foreign participation in petrochemical industries and on the particular type of contractual arrangement used in different countries.

Tables 4-8 and 4-9 provide survey data by country on the type of technology agreement used and the degree of local and foreign ownership of recipient entities. The tables show similar but not identical patterns. In table 4-8, Chile and Argentina have the largest proportion of plants with technology agreements permitting foreign control, followed by Colombia, which has the largest proportion of subsidiaries. At the other end of the spectrum, apart from the very small Peruvian sample, Venezuela and Mexico have the largest proportion of plants under local control, with Brazil in third place. Mexico has the largest proportion of SLAS.

In table 4-9, Venezuela, Peru, and Mexico have the largest proportions of plants with majority local ownership. Peru, followed by Mexico, has the largest proportion of wholly locally owned plants. Argentina and Colombia have the largest proportions of plants under predominantly foreign ownership, with Brazil in third place. Detailed data by product subgroups not reproduced here show that all countries but Argentina and Peru obtained the technology for plants manufacturing basic products through SLAS; for intermediate and final products, Argentina and Colombia had the largest proportions of technology agreements permitting transfers through subsidiaries of foreign firms.

These results broadly reflect the discussion in chapter 3, which showed that Mexico had a strong and relatively old regulatory framework limiting foreign ownership, together with relatively highly developed indigenous technological capacity and a powerful state enterprise which reserved basic and some intermediate products to itself; that foreign private firms had played a major role in Argentina's petrochemical industry in the early 1970s; that Brazil, like Mexico, had a strong state enterprise but was more inclined than Mexico to permit some degree of foreign ownership in plants manufacturing all three product groups; and that Venezuela, with a small number of relatively large plants, had initially developed its petrochemical industry under the auspices of its state enterprise with the maximum degree of unpackaging.

Table 4-8. Relationship between Recipient Country and Type of Technology Agreement: 280 Petrochemical Plants

Recipient country	(a) Local technology		(b) Straight license (SLA)		(c) Minority participation		(d) Local control (a) + (b) + (c)		(e) Shared participation	
	Number	Percent	Number	Percent	Number	Percent	Number	Percent	Number	Percent
Argentina	2	4	24	53	5	11	31	69	0	0
Brazil	0	0	40	57	17	24	57	81	1	1
Chile	1	10	5	50	0	0	6	60	0	0
Colombia	0	0	14	64	1	5	15	68	1	5
Mexico	0	0	47	78	8	13	55	92	0	0
Peru	0	0	6	68	1	14	7	100	0	0
Venezuela	0	0	12	67	5	28	17	94	0	0
Total	3	1	148	64	37	16	188	81	2	1

Recipient country	(f) Majority participation		(g) Subsidiary		(h) Licensor control (f) + (g)		(i) All known (d) + (e) + (h)		(j) Licensor participation, extent unknown	(k) Participation not known	(l) Total number (i) + (j) + (k)
	Number	Percent	Number	Percent	Number	Percent	Number	Percent			
Argentina	5	11	9	20	14	31	45	100	0	6	51
Brazil	4	6	8	11	12	17	70	100	0	10	80
Chile	3	30	1	10	4	40	10	100	1	3	13
Colombia	0	0	6	27	6	27	22	100	2	4	28
Mexico	0	0	5	8	5	8	60	100	1	7	68
Peru	0	0	0	0	0	0	7	100	0	12	19
Venezuela	0	0	1	6	1	6	18	100	0	3	21
Total	12	5	30	13	42	18	232	100	3	45	280

Note: All percentages are proportions of row subtotals in column (i); items may not add to totals because of rounding.

Table 4-9. *Relationship between Recipient Country and Degree of Local and Foreign Ownership: 280 Petrochemical Plants*

Recipient country	(a) Wholly local		(b) Foreign minority		(c) Local control (a + b)		(d) Shared ownership		(e) Foreign majority	
	Number	Percent	Number	Percent	Number	Percent	Number	Percent	Number	Percent
Argentina	15	30	8	16	23	46	0	0	9	18
Brazil	18	24	25	33	43	57	3	4	13	17
Chile	9	69	0	0	9	69	0	0	3	23
Colombia	11	42	1	4	12	46	1	4	2	8
Mexico	44	70	13	21	57	90	0	0	0	0
Peru	17	89	1	5	18	95	0	0	0	0
Venezuela	11	52	9	43	20	95	0	0	0	0
Total	125	47	57	21	182	68	4	1	27	10

Recipient country	(f) Subsidiary		(g) Foreign control (e) + (f)		(h) All known (c) + (d) + (g)		(i) Foreign ownership, extent unknown	(j) Ownership not known	(k) Total number (h) + (i) + (j)
	Number	Percent	Number	Percent	Number	Percent			
Argentina	18	36	27	54	50	100	0	1	51
Brazil	17	22	30	39	76	100	2	2	80
Chile	1	8	4	31	13	100	0	0	13
Colombia	11	42	13	50	26	100	2	0	28
Mexico	6	10	6	10	63	100	3	2	68
Peru	1	5	1	5	19	100	0	0	19
Venezuela	1	5	1	5	21	100	0	0	21
Total	55	21	82	31	268	100	7	5	280

Note: All percentages are proportions of row subtotals in column (h); items may not add to totals because of rounding.

Statistical tests of the data showed that errors in predicting the type of agreement used for transferring the technology for basic and final products could be significantly reduced if the recipient country was known. Thus, for these two product subgroups at least, country variations do indeed seem to influence the incidence of different types of contractual agreement.

Suppliers' Country

Table 2-10 provided a breakdown of the types of transfer agreement signed by individual suppliers who were producers, and table 3-7 summarized these agreements by country of origin. Although individual suppliers appeared to be relatively flexible in the type of contractual arrangement they used for transfer, statistical testing showed that the likelihood of error in predicting the type of arrangement used was reduced if the name of the supplier was known. A question with wider implications is whether the types of contractual arrangement used vary systematically by country of origin of the suppliers of petrochemical technology.

Aggregate data on the relationship between the countries of origin of suppliers who are producers and types of contractual agreement have already been discussed in chapter 3. Table 4-10 subdivides these supplier country data by the time periods in which agreements were signed—pre-1960, 1960–69, since 1970, and unknown—by type of agreement, and by whether there was *any* licensor participation (column j) on the ground that suppliers can influence policies even with only minority participation.

Taking the supplier countries with relatively large numbers of agreements, the table shows that the four largest sources of technology (the United States, Germany, France, and the United Kingdom) tended to have the most restrictive licensing policies, although the much smaller Belgian sample did include two subsidiaries, and most Dutch transfers included minority participation. The United States was by far the largest source of agreements overall (a total of 64 of the 124 agreements between producer suppliers in developed countries and Latin American recipients) and accounted for the largest proportion of agreements involving some degree of participation (51 agreements, or 80 percent of all those entered into by U.S. firms). Germany, the second largest source of agreements, also scored high in terms of the overall proportion of agreements with Latin American recipients involving supplier participation (67 percent). In the case of French and British producers (who tied for third place in number of agreements), 67 percent and 56 percent respectively of agreements signed involved some degree of supplier participation. But for each of these countries, the proportion of agreements involving some degree of participation has been declining in recent years: for the United States, from 100 percent for agreements signed before 1960 to 74 percent in the 1960–69 period to 71 percent since 1969; for Germany from 100 percent to 50 percent to 33 percent over the same three time periods; in the cases of France and the United Kingdom from 100 percent and 75 percent respectively in the 1960–69 period to 80 percent and 50 percent respectively since 1969. These data further confirm the trend noted earlier of a decline in producer-suppliers' requirements for extensive participation in recipients' post-start-up activities. Nevertheless, statistical tests of the data confirmed the existence of a relationship between country of origin of the technology and type of technology agreement.

Conclusion

The reader who has persevered up to this point will, it is hoped, need little persuading that the world of technology transfer is not an economic determinist's morality play, in which all issues are clear-cut and involve straightforward conflicts between the righteous and the self-serving. Rather, the observer of the scene is faced by a complex and constantly changing landscape, composed in contrasting shades of grey, not stark blacks and whites, in which some time must be spent before the analytical retina is capable of discerning the subtle and shifting patterns and contrasts which make up the picture as a whole. One of the major difficulties in reading (and writing) about the subject is precisely its fluidity and ambiguity; generalized prescriptions will not do—however attractive to policymakers who would prefer the easy confrontation to the complex compromise.

Thus it is neither easy nor appropriate to draw hard and fast conclusions from the data collected. Every statement needs qualification. Nevertheless, the findings presented in this chapter suggest (and a multivariate analysis of variance not reproduced here confirms) that

- The main determinants of the type of contractual arrangements used in petrochemical technology transfers to Latin America are, in order of importance, type of product, recipients' country, and suppliers' country.
- Product and process maturity factors are not significant in determining the type of technology agreement used.

Table 4-10. *Relationship between Supplier's Country of Origin and Type of Technology Agreement, by Age of Plant: 124 Petrochemical Plants Using Technology Supplied by Foreign Producer Companies*

Supplier's country and age of plant[a]	(a) Straight license (SLA)		(b) Foreign minority		(c) Local control (a) + (b)		(d) Shared participation		(e) Foreign majority	
	Number	Percent	Number	Percent	Number	Percent	Number	Percent	Number	Percent
United States										
Pre-1960	0	0	1	17	1	17	0	0	3	50
1960–69	7	27	5	19	12	46	2	8	3	12
Post-1969	6	30	10	50	16	80	0	0	3	15
All known	13	25	16	31	29	56	2	4	9	17
Date unknown	0	0	1	11	1	11	0	0	1	11
Total	13	21	17	28	30	49	2	3	10	16
Germany, Fed. Repub. of										
Pre-1960	0	0	0	0	0	0	0	0	1	50
1960–69	2	50	1	25	3	75	0	0	0	0
Post-1969	2	67	1	33	3	100	0	0	0	0
All known	4	44	2	22	6	67	0	0	1	11
Date unknown	0	0	0	0	0	0	0	0	0	0
Total	4	33	2	17	6	50	0	0	1	8
France										
Pre-1960	1	100	0	0	1	100	0	0	0	0
1960–69	0	0	0	0	0	0	0	0	1	30
Post-1969	1	20	3	60	4	80	0	0	0	0
All known	2	25	3	38	5	63	0	0	1	13
Date unknown	1	100	0	0	1	100	0	0	0	0
Total	3	33	3	33	6	67	0	0	1	11

United Kingdom														
Pre-1960	1	100	0	0	1	100	0	0	0	0	0	0	0	0
1960–69	1	25	2	30	3	75	0	0	0	0	0	0	0	0
Post-1969	2	50	2	50	4	100	0	0	0	0	0	0	0	0
Total	4	44	4	44	8	89	0	0	0	0	0	0	0	0
Italy														
Pre-1960	1	100	0	0	1	100	0	0	0	0	0	0	0	0
1960–69	6	86	1	14	7	100	0	0	0	0	0	0	0	0
Post-1969	0	0	0	0	0	0	0	0	0	0	0	0	0	0
Total	7	88	1	13	8	100	0	0	0	0	0	0	0	0
Japan														
Pre-1960	0	0	0	0	0	0	0	0	0	0	0	0	0	0
1960–69	0	0	0	0	0	0	0	0	0	0	0	0	0	0
Post-1969	4	57	3	43	7	100	0	0	0	0	0	0	0	0
Total	4	57	3	43	7	100	0	0	0	0	0	0	0	0
Holland														
Pre-1960	0	0	0	0	0	0	0	0	0	0	0	0	0	0
1960–69	1	100	0	0	1	100	0	0	0	0	0	0	0	0
Post-1969	0	0	4	100	4	100	0	0	0	0	0	0	0	0
Total	1	20	4	80	5	100	0	0	0	0	0	0	0	0
Belgium														
Pre-1960	0	0	0	0	0	0	0	0	0	0	0	0	0	0
1960–69	1	100	0	0	1	100	0	0	0	0	0	0	0	0
Post-1969	0	0	1	50	1	50	0	0	0	0	0	0	0	0
Total	1	25	1	25	2	50	0	0	0	0	0	0	0	0

(Table continues on the following page.)

Table 4-10 (continued)

Supplier's country and age of plant[a]	(f) Subsidiary		(g) Licensor control (e) + (f)		(h) All known (c) + (d) + (g)		(i) Foreign participation, extent unknown	(j) All foreign participation (h) + (i) − (a)		(k) Owner-ship not known	(l) Total number (a) + (k) (i) + (k)
	Number	Percent	Number	Percent	Number	Percent	known	Number	Percent	known	
United States											
Pre-1960	2	33	5	83	6	100	0	6	100	0	6
1960–69	9	35	12	46	26	100	1	20	74	0	27
Post-1969	1	5	4	20	20	100	1	15	71	0	21
All known	12	23	21	40	52	100	2	41	76	0	54
Date unknown	7	78	8	89	9	100	1	10	100	0	10
Total	19	31	29	48	61	100	3	51	80	0	64
Germany, Fed. Repub. of											
Pre-1960	1	50	2	100	2	100	0	2	100	0	2
1960–69	1	25	1	50	4	100	0	2	50	0	4
Post-1969	0	0	0	0	3	100	0	1	33	0	3
All known	2	22	3	33	9	100	0	5	56	0	9
Date unknown	3	100	3	100	3	100	0	3	100	0	3
Total	5	42	6	50	12	100	0	8	67	0	12
France											
Pre-1960	0	0	0	0	1	100	0	0	0	0	1
1960–69	1	50	2	100	2	100	0	2	100	0	2
Post-1969	1	20	1	20	5	100	0	4	80	0	5
All known	2	25	3	38	8	100	0	6	75	0	8
Date unknown	0	0	0	0	1	100	0	0	0	0	1
Total	2	22	3	33	9	100	0	6	67	0	9

136

(Table continues on the following page.)

United Kingdom

Pre-1960	0	0	0	0	1	100	0	0	0	0	1
1960–69	1	25	1	25	4	100	0	3	75	0	4
Post-1969	0	0	0	0	4	100	0	2	50	0	4
Total	1	11	1	11	9	100	0	5	56	0	9

Italy

Pre-1960	0	0	0	0	1	100	0	0	0	0	1
1960–69	0	0	0	0	7	100	0	1	14	0	7
Post-1969	0	0	0	0	0	0	0	0	0	0	0
Total	0	0	0	0	8	100	0	1	13	0	8

Japan

Pre-1960	0	0	0	0	0	0	0	0	0	0	0
1960–69	0	0	0	0	0	0	0	0	0	0	0
Post-1969	0	0	0	0	7	100	0	3	43	0	7
Total	0	0	0	0	7	100	0	3	43	0	7

Holland

Pre-1960	0	0	0	0	0	0	0	0	0	0	0
1960–69	0	0	0	0	1	100	0	0	0	0	1
Post-1969	0	0	0	0	4	100	0	4	80	1	5
Total	0	0	0	0	5	100	0	4	67	1	6

Belgium

Pre-1960	1	100	1	100	1	100	0	1	100	0	1
1960–69	0	0	0	0	1	100	0	0	0	0	1
Post-1969	1	50	1	50	2	100	0	0	0	0	2
Total	2	50	2	50	4	100	0	3	75	0	4

Table 4-10 (continued)

Supplier's country and age of plant[a]	(a) Straight license (SLA)		(b) Foreign minority		(c) Local control (a) + (b)		(d) Shared participation		(e) Foreign majority	
	Number	Percent	Number	Percent	Number	Percent	Number	Percent	Number	Percent
Sweden										
Pre-1960	0	0	0	0	0	0	0	0	0	0
1960–69	1	100	0	0	1	100	0	0	0	0
Post-1969	2	100	0	0	2	100	0	0	0	0
Total	3	100	0	0	3	100	0	0	0	0
Austria										
Pre-1960	1	100	0	0	1	100	0	0	0	0
Total	1	100	0	0	1	100	0	0	0	0
Canada										
1960–69	0	0	1	100	1	100	0	0	0	0
Total	0	0	1	100	1	100	0	0	0	0
All foreign suppliers										
Pre-1960	4	31	1	8	5	38	0	0	4	31
1960–69	19	40	10	21	29	62	2	4	4	9
Post-1969	17	36	24	51	41	87	0	0	3	6
All known	40	37	35	33	75	70	2	2	11	20
Date unknown	1	8	1	8	2	15	0	0	1	8
All plants	41	34	36	30	77	64	2	2	12	10

Supplier's country and age of plant[a]	(f) Subsidiary		(g) Licensor control (e) + (f)		(h) All known (c) + (d) + (g)		(i) Foreign participation, extent unknown	(j) All foreign participation (h) + (i) − (a)		(k) Ownership not known	(l) Total number (a) + (j) + (k)
	Number	Percent	Number	Percent	Number	Percent		Number	Percent		
Sweden											
Pre-1960	0	0	0	0	0	0	0	0	0	0	0
1960–69	0	0	0	0	1	100	0	0	0	0	1
Post-1969	0	0	0	0	2	100	0	0	0	0	2
Total	0	0	0	0	3	100	0	0	0	0	3
Austria											
Pre-1960	0	0	0	0	1	100	0	0	0	0	1
Total	0	0	0	0	1	100	0	0	0	0	1
Canada											
1960–69	0	0	0	0	1	100	0	1	100	0	1
Total	0	0	0	0	1	100	0	1	100	0	1
All foreign suppliers											
Pre-1960	4	31	8	62	13	100	0	9	69	0	13
1960–69	12	26	16	34	47	100	1	29	60	0	48
Post-1969	3	6	6	13	47	100	1	31	63	1	49
All known	19	18	30	28	107	100	2	69	63	0	110
Date unknown	10	77	11	84	13	100	1	13	93	0	14
All plants	29	24	41	34	120	100	3	82	66	1	124

Note: All percentages except those in column (j) are proportions of row subtotals in column (h); percentages in column (j) are proportions of totals shown in column (l).

a. Age of plant refers to the period of construction.

- The terms of transfer appear to have become more liberal in recent years as nonproducer-suppliers have increased their share of transfers and as producers have developed flexible responses to recipient countries' legislation restricting foreign participation.

That having been said, three important caveats need to be made. First, the data presented here cannot be used to prove that maturity factors play no part in the contractual arrangements for technology transfers generally. There are major differences between transfers from one developed country to another on the one hand and those from developed to developing countries on the other, and the petrochemical industry has a number of characteristics which make it something of a special case. Second, the apparent "liberalization" of transfer arrangements in recent years observed from the data does not necessarily mean that suppliers' actual influence over recipients is commensurately reduced; the licensor can often retain significant involvement in the recipient's affairs, even if he is only a minority shareholder. Third, the extent to which this involvement remains may reflect recipients' as well as suppliers' perceptions that their interests are served by its retention.

To sum up, it would be wrong to extend the descriptive findings presented here into a series of general policy prescriptions, because these would fail to do justice to the complex reality of technology transfer arrangements in the petrochemical industry and the institutional framework within which they take place in Latin America. This book has been avowedly descriptive. It will have served its purpose if it has given the reader a little more information about the what, who, how, and why of technology transfers in the Latin American petrochemical industry— and if it has demonstrated the complex and changing nature of the influences determining the form and structure of individual technology transfer transactions, in a world of conditional probability rather than of absolute prescription.

Note

1. As in chapter 2, Goodman and Kruskal's Tau A and B have been used to test the strength of relationships (see chapter 2, note 9).

Appendixes

APPENDIX A
Ownership Structure and Capacity of Selected Petrochemical Plants in Seven Latin American Countries

Table A-1. *Argentina*
(capacity in thousands of metric tons a year)

Ownership	Existing plants		Engineering and construction		Planning		Total	
	Number	Capacity	Number	Capacity	Number	Capacity	Number	Capacity
Basic products								
Locally owned	3	88	—	—	—	—	3	88
Minority foreign	2	36	1	200	—	—	3	236
Majority foreign	2	94	—	—	—	23[a]	2	117
Subsidiary	6	242	—	200[a]	—	20[a]	6	462
Total	13	460	1	400	—	43	14	903
Intermediate products								
Locally owned	4	82	2	126	2	29	8	237
Minority foreign	2	33	—	—	1	100	3	133
Majority foreign	3	76	—	—	1	27	4	103
Foreign unknown	—	—	—	—	1	35	1	35
Subsidiary	5	93	—	10[a]	—	—	5	103
Total	14	284	2	136	5	191	21	611
Final products								
Locally owned	2	10	—	—	1	30	3	40
Minority foreign	1	28	1	55	—	30[a]	2	113
Majority foreign	3	47	—	30[a]	—	—	3	77
Subsidiary	7	157	—	—	—	—	7	157
Total	13	242	1	85	1	60	15	387

Table A-2. *Brazil*
(capacity in thousands of metric tons a year)

Ownership	Existing plants		Engineering and construction		Planning		Total	
	Number	Capacity	Number	Capacity	Number	Capacity	Number	Capacity
Basic products								
Locally owned	8	331	2	397	—	—	10	728
Minority foreign	3	471	3	565	—	—	6	1,036
Shared control	1	14	—	—	—	—	1	14
Majority foreign	2	218	—	—	—	—	2	218
Subsidiary	3	29	—	—	—	—	3	29
Total	17	1063	5	962	—	—	22	2,025
Intermediate products								
Locally owned	6	112	2	324	—	—	8	436
Minority foreign	3	65	4	263	2	104	9	432
Majority foreign	7	264	1	106	1	60	9	430
Subsidiary	6	133	—	15[a]	1	150	7	298
Total	22	574	7	708	4	314	33	1,596
Final products								
Locally owned	1	75	—	35	—	—	1	110
Minority foreign	3	141	4	252	2	150	9	543
Shared control	2	52	—	—	—	—	2	52
Majority foreign	1	26	1	40	—	—	1	26
Foreign unknown	1	4	—	—	—	—	2	44
Subsidiary	5	214	3	85	—	—	8	299
Total	13	512	8	412	2	150	23	1,074

a. Expansion of an existing plant.

143

Table A-3. *Chile*
(capacity in thousands of metric tons a year)

Ownership	Existing plants		Planning		Total	
	Number	*Capacity*	*Number*	*Capacity*	*Number*	*Capacity*
Basic products						
Locally owned	3	110	1	330	4	440
Total	3	110	1	330	4	440
Intermediate products						
Locally owned	2	25	2	325	4	350
Majority foreign	1	18	—	—	1	18
Total	3	43	2	325	5	368
Final products						
Locally owned	—	—	1	50	1	50
Majority foreign	2	35	—	—	2	35
Subsidiary	1	6	—	—	1	6
Total	3	41	1	50	4	91

Table A-4. Colombia
(capacity in thousands of metric tons a year)

Ownership	Existing plants		Engineering and construction		Planning		Total	
	Number	Capacity	Number	Capacity	Number	Capacity	Number	Capacity
Basic products								
Locally owned	4	388	1	11	1	100	6	499
Subsidiary	2ª	117	—	—	—	—	2	117
Total	6	505	1	11	1	100	8	616
Intermediate products								
Locally owned	3	167	1	16	1	50	5	233
Majority foreign	2ᵇ	89	—	—	—	—	2	89
Foreign unknown	1	12	—	—	—	—	1	12
Subsidiary	5	24	—	—	—	—	5	24
Total	11	292	1	16	1	50	13	358
Final products								
Locally owned	—	—	1	45	—	—	1	45
Minority foreign	1	9	—	—	—	—	1	9
Shared control	1	19	—	6	—	—	1	25
Majority foreign	1	22	—	—	—	—	1	22
Subsidiary	4	38	—	7	—	—	4	45
Total	7	88	1	58	—	—	8	146

a. Changed to local ownership.
b. A plant of 72 metric tons a year changed to local ownership.

Table A-5. *Mexico*
(capacity in thousands of metric tons a year)

Ownership	Existing plants		Engineering and construction		Planning		Total	
	Number	Capacity	Number	Capacity	Number	Capacity	Number	Capacity
Basic products								
Locally owned	11	1,262	7	2,372	—	—	18	3,634
Total	11	1,262	7	2,372	—	—	18	3,634
Intermediate products								
Locally owned	14	775	4	520	3	300	21	1,595
Minority foreign	7	193	1	111	—	—	8	304
Subsidiary	1	5	—	—	—	—	1	5
Total	22	973	5	631	3	300	30	1,904
Final products								
Locally owned	2	75	—	—	2	280	4	355
Minority foreign	5	147	1	40	—	—	6	187
Majority foreign	3	25	—	—	—	—	3	25
Foreign unknown	2	6	—	—	—	—	2	6
Subsidiary	3	43	—	—	—	—	3	43
Total	15	296	1	40	2	280	18	616

Table A-6. *Peru*
(capacity in thousands of metric tons a year)

Ownership	Existing plants		Planning		Total	
	Number	Capacity	Number	Capacity	Number	Capacity
Basic products						
Locally owned	2	113	2	225	4	368
Minority foreign	1	25	—	—	1	25
Total	3	138	2	255	5	393
Intermediate products						
Locally owned	1	168	6	257	7	425
Total	1	168	6	257	7	425
Final products						
Locally owned	—	—	6[a]	288	6	288
Subsidiary	1[b]	7	—	—	1	7
Total	1	7	6	288	7	295

a. Some will probably become joint venture with minority foreign participation.
b. Now locally owned (government).

Table A-7. *Venezuela*
(capacity in thousands of metric tons a year)

Ownership	Existing plants		Engineering and construction		Planning		Total	
	Number	*Capacity*	*Number*	*Capacity*	*Number*	*Capacity*	*Number*	*Capacity*
Basic products								
Locally owned	3	403	—	—	1	178	4	581
Minority foreign	1	590	—	—	1	590	2	1180
Total	4	993	—	—	2	768	6	1761
Intermediate products								
Locally owned	5	290	—	—	—	—	5	290
Minority foreign	3	826	1	52	—	—	4	878
Total	8	1116	1	52	—	—	9	1168
Final products								
Locally owned	—	—	—	—	2	150	2	150
Minority foreign	2	64	1	70	—	—	3	134
Subsidiary	1	10	—	—	—	—	1	10
Total	3	74	1	70	2	150	6	294

APPENDIX B. *Biggest Plants in Latin America*
(capacity in thousands of metric tons a year)

Product	Developed-country norm[a]	Country	Built	Engineering or under construction	Planning stage
Basic products					
Ethylene	1960 (Europe):	Argentina	85	200	—
	40	Brazil	310	384	—
	1970–75	Chile	60	—	—
	(Europe):	Colombia	20	—	100
	400	Mexico	182	500	—
		Peru	160	—	—
		Venezuela	150	—	—
Benzene	1970–75:	Argentina	70	70	—
	160	Brazil	111	129	—
		Chile	—	—	—
		Colombia	45	—	—
		Mexico	70	295	—
		Peru	—	—	95
Butadiene	1960: 50	Argentina	36	66[b]	—
	1970–75: 100	Brazil	65	75[b]	—
		Colombia	10	—	—
		Mexico	50	55	—
Ammonia	1960: 80	Argentina	68	—	—
	1973–75	Brazil	198	300	—
	500	Chile	—	330	—
		Colombia	300	—	—
		Mexico	330	890[b]	—
		Peru	100	—	—
		Venezuela	590	—	590[b]
Methanol	1975: 400	Argentina	33	—	—
		Brazil	30	51	—
		Mexico	22	150	—
		Venezuela	—	—	178
Intermediate products					
Acetaldehyde	—	Brazil	40	—	60
		Chile	25	—	—
		Mexico	100	—	—
Acrylonitrile	1960: 45	Argentina	—	—	9
	1970–75: 135	Brazil	—	—	60
		Mexico	24	—	—
		Peru	—	—	50
Caprolactam	—	Argentina	—	—	35
		Brazil	—	35	—
		Colombia	17	—	—
		Mexico	41	—	—
		Peru	—	—	16

(Table continues on the following page.)

APPENDIX B *(continued)*

Product	Developed-country norm[a]	Country	Built	Engineering or under construction	Planning stage
Cyclohexane	1960: 60	Argentina	45	—	—
	1970–75: 150	Brazil	—	—	44
		Colombia	21	—	—
		Mexico	100	—	—
Dimethyl terephthalate (DMT)	—	Argentina	14	—	—
		Brazil	—	60	—
		Colombia	—	—	50
		Mexico	—	91	—
Dodecylbenzene	—	Argentina	10	91	—
		Brazil	27	—	—
		Colombia	—	16	—
		Mexico	26	—	50
		Venezuela	18	—	—
Ethylene oxide	1960: 45	Argentina	19	—	—
		Brazil	35	100[b]	—
		Mexico	24	100	—
Formaldehyde	1970–75: 90	Argentina	19	—	—
		Brazil	43	30	—
		Chile	20	—	—
		Colombia	9	—	—
		Mexico	8	—	—
		Venezuela	10	—	—
Phenol	1960: 25	Argentina	10	35	—
		Brazil	51	—	—
		Mexico	25	—	—
Phthalic anhydride	1960: 15	Argentina	12	22	—
	1970–75: 45	Brazil	18	24[b]	—
		Colombia	5	—	—
		Mexico	10	—	—
		Peru	10	—	—
		Venezuela	18	—	—
Isopropanol	1960: 50	Argentina	18	—	—
	1970–75: 220	Brazil	4	—	—
		Mexico	24	—	—
		Peru	—	—	11
Styrene	1960: 45	Argentina	50	—	—
	1970–75: 450	Brazil	60	100	—
		Mexico	35	100	—
		Peru	—	—	90

Product	Developed-country norm[a]	Country	Built	Engineering or under construction	Planning stage
Vinyl chloride	1960: 135	Argentina	—	—	100
monomer (VCM)		Brazil	200	—	150
		Chile	18	—	—
		Colombia	12	—	—
		Mexico	77	—	150
		Peru	—	—	80
		Venezuela	—	50	—
Urea	—	Argentina	55	—	—
		Brazil	82	264	—
		Chile	—	—	300
		Colombia	130	—	—
		Mexico	267	300	—
		Peru	168	—	—
		Venezuela	790	—	—
Final products					
Low-density	1970–75: 200	Argentina	30	55	—
polyethylene		Brazil	88	100	—
(LDPE)		Chile	20	—	—
		Colombia	19	45	—
		Mexico	51	1	180
		Peru	—	—	90
		Venezuela	50	—	—
High-density	1970–75: 150	Brazil	10	60	—
polyethylene		Colombia	—	—	30
(HDPE)		Mexico	—	—	100
		Peru	—	—	30
		Venezuela	—	—	100
Polystyrene	—	Argentina	28	—	—
		Brazil	26	45	—
		Chile	6	—	—
		Colombia	6	13[b]	—
		Mexico	20	40	—
		Venezuela	14	38[b]	—
Polyvinyl chloride	—	Argentina	20	—	58
(PVC)		Brazil	43	—	140
		Chile	15	—	—
		Colombia	22	—	—
		Mexico	22	—	—
		Peru	7	—	70
		Venezuela	—	46	—

(Table continues on the following page.)

APPENDIX B *(continued)*

Product	Developed-country norm[a]	Country	Built	Engineering or under construction	Planning stage
Styrene butadiene rubber (SBR)	—	Argentina	50	—	—
		Brazil	75	110[b]	—
		Mexico	49	—	—
		Peru	—	—	60
		Venezuela	—	—	20
Polypropylene	—	Argentina	25	—	30
		Brazil	—	50	—
		Chile	—	—	50
		Peru	—	—	30
		Venezuela	—	—	50
Carbon black	—	Argentina	42	—	—
		Brazil	43	56[b]	—
		Colombia	14	—	—
		Mexico	40	—	—
		Peru	—	—	8
		Venezuela	10	—	—

a. The average capacity in developed countries for the years shown. These developed-country norms for size of plants are taken from *Revue de l'IFP* (Institut Français du Pétrole, May-June 1972).

b. Expansion of the same plant that appears under "Built."

APPENDIX C. *Agents Involved in a Group of Selected Petrochemical Projects in Latin America*

Firm and country	Type of firm	Signature contracts	Licensor	Basic engineering
Venoco (Venezuela)	JVGLF⁻ F = 15%	1966	Phillips (U.S.)	Pona Engineering (U.S.) *Payment*: fixed price
Monómeros (Venezuela and Colombia)	JVGGF⁻ F = 8.18%	1968	Stamicarbon (Netherlands)	Stamicarbon
Estizulia (Venezuela)	JVGLF⁻ F = 25%	1971	Dart Industries (U.S.)	Dart Industries
Polilago (Venezuela)	JVGF⁻ F = 30%	1971	Ethylene Plastique (France)	Ethylene Plastique
Petroplas (Venezuela)	JVGF⁻ F = 25%	1973	B. F. Goodrich (U.S.)	B. F. Goodrich
Tripoliven (Venezuela)	JVGLF⁻ F = 33%	1973	FMC (U.S.) Foret (Spain)	Foret
Produven (Venezuela)	JVG/F F = 50%	1973	Pechiney Ugine Kulhman (PCUK, France) Rhodafin (France)	PCUK
Carbocloro (Argentina)	GL	1963	Rheinprenheusen (Germany)	Rheinprenheusen
Cia Pernanbucana de Borracha (Brazil)	GL	1961	Union Carbide (Germany); butadiene Firestone (U.S.); polybutadiene	Firestone (U.S.) Lummus (France)
Negromex (Mexico)	JVGLF⁻ F = 10%	1961	Phillips (U.S.)	Phillips (also equipment design)
Policolsa (Colombia)	JVG/F F = 50%	1961	Dow Chemicals (U.S.)	Dow Chemicals
Ferralca (Venezuela)	GL	1972	Continho Caro (Germany)	Continho Caro *Payment*: fixed sum
Petrosur (Argentina)	F	1961	n.a.	Chemical Construction Corp. (U.S.)[bc]
Enap (Chile)	G	1967	Lummus (France) and Lummus (U.S.)	Lummus (France)

(Table continues on the following page.)

APPENDIX C (*continued*)

Firm and country	Detailed engineering	Procure- ment
Venoco (Venezuela)	Eclipse Engineering (U.S.) *Payment*: fixed price	Foreign equipment = 52% Local equipment = 48%
Monómeros (Venezuela and Colombia)	McKee—CTIP (U.S.)	Equipment linked with financing
Estizulia (Venezuela)	Ortloff (U.S.) *Payment*: cost plus[a]	Ortloff *Payment*: cost plus *Equipment*: mainly U.S.
Polilago (Venezuela)	Coppee Rust (Belgium; licensee of Ethylene Plastique) *Payment*: fixed price for engineering and equipment	Coppee Rust *Payment*: fixed sum *Equipment Supplier*: Société Général d'Entreprise S.A. (France)
Petroplas (Venezuela)	*Engineering*: Badger France (Subsidiary of Badger, U.S.) *General contractor*: Creusot-Loire (France) *Payment*: fixed sum for engineering and equipment	Creusot-Loire *Equipment*: France 75% Venezuela 15% Other 10%
Tripoliven (Venezuela)	IPEC-VEN (France and Venezuela) *Subcontractors*: Export Life Engineering Haifa (Israel) *Payment*: fixed sum	IPEC-VEN *Equipment*: Spain Venezuela
Produven (Venezuela)	PCUK *Payment*: guaranteed maximum engineering fee based on hours worked	PCUK
Carbocloro (Argentina)	Mellor Goodwin (Argentina)	*International procurement*: Lurgi (Germany); equipment manufacturing and quality control, supervision of delivery and timing *Local procurement*: Mellor Goodwin

Firm and country	Other services	Financing
Venoco (Venezuela)	*Civil engineering*: local *Assembly*: local	CVF (government agency)
Monómeros (Venezuela and Colombia)	n.a.	U.S. banks European banks
Estizulia (Venezuela)	*Local contractors*:[a] Formiconi y Ley (Venezuela) and others for civil works, assembly, and electrical engineering	n.a.
Polilago (Venezuela)	*Construction*: Coppee Rust (subsidiary in Venezuela) *Assembly*: Formiconi y Ley (Venezuela)	Banque de Paris et des Pays Bas (France) Paribas (France and Belgium) Inarco Investment (Netherlands)
Petroplas (Venezuela)	*Assembly*: Ditsa and Spie Batignole (both French; associated with Creusot-Loire) *Civil works*: local *Electrical works*: local	Banque de Suez et de l'Union des Mines (France) Banque Français du Commerce Extérieur (France) Crédit Lyonnais (France) American Express International Banking (U.S.)
Tripoliven (Venezuela)	*Civil engineering*: Ingenieria Rubinstein (Venezuela)	International Marine Banking (U.S.)
Produven (Venezuela)	n.a.	Banque de Suez et de l'Union des Mines (France) Banque Français du Commerce Extérieur (France) Crédit Lyonnais (France)
Carbocloro (Argentina)	*Engineering of local works*: Carbocloro	Inter-American Development Bank Local financing

(Table continues on the following page.)

APPENDIX C (continued)

Firm and country	Detailed engineering	Procure-ment
Cia Pernanbucana de Borracha (Brazil)	Lummus (France)	Lummus (France) *Payment*: fixed fee for dismantling and packing used butadiene unit *Equipment*: Rohm and Hass (U.S.; used plant)
Negromex (Mexico)	Pona Engineering (U.S.)	n.a.
Policolsa (Colombia) Ferralca (Venezuela)	Dow Chemicals *Payment*: fixed sum Continho Caro *Payment*: fixed sum[b]	Dow Chemicals *Payment*: fixed sum *Procurement in Germany*: Continho Caro *Payment*: fixed sum *Local procurement*: Ritec (Venezuela)
Petrosur (Argentina)	Chemical Construction Corp.	*Procurement abroad*: Chemical Construction Corp. *Local procurement*: Techint (Italy and Argentina) Local equipment = 45%
Enap (Chile)	Lummus (France) *Payment*: guaranteed maximum basis; engineering fee based on hours worked	*Procurement*: Lummus (France) *Equipment*: 75% in France, Italy, Germany, U.K.; 25% in U.S.

Firm and country	Other services	Financing
Cia Pernanbucana de Borracha (Brazil)	*Plant management agreement*: Firestone *Construction*: Lummus (France) *Contractor*: Montreal (Brazil)	Comptoir d'Escompt de Paris (France) Crédit Lyonnais (France) Inter-American Development Bank AID/Alliance for Progress Suppliers' credits (Rohm and Hass) BNDE (Brazil)
Negromex (Mexico)	*Contractor*: Negromex	Inter-American Development Bank Local banks
Policolsa (Colombia)	*Contractor*: McKee/CTIP (U.S.)	n.a.
Ferralca (Venezuela)	*Contractor*: Ritec (Venezuela) for civil engineering, supervision of assembly, civil works, receiving and checking French equipment, and personnel training *Payment*: fixed sum	Bankers' Trust (U.S.)
Petrosur (Argentina)	*Local contractor*: Techint (co-ordination of works) *Feasibility studies*: Ebasco Services (U.S.; associated with Chemical Construction Corp.)	Inter-American Development Bank
Enap (Chile)	n.a.	Inter-American Development Bank Others

n.a. Not available.

Key: JV = joint ventures; G = public enterprises; L = local private firms; F = foreign firms; + = majority participation; − = minority participation; / = shared participation; ? = unknown.

a. Contract renegotiated; originally a lump-sum contract.

b. Engineering and equipment in one item.

c. Links between Chemical Construction Corp. and American and Foreign Power which has 51.9 percent of the shares.

Bibliography

The word "processed" describes works that are reproduced from typescript by mimeograph, xerography, or similar means; such works may not be cataloged or commonly available through libraries, or may be subject to restricted circulation.

Transfer of Technology and Technology Policies

Añez, C. "International Transfer of Technology for Oil and Gas Exploration and Production: The Case of the Venezuelan Oil Industry." D.Phil. dissertation, University of Sussex, 1980.

Añez, C. "Technological Elaboration of an Industrial Investment." Preliminary draft, Science Policy Research Unit, University of Sussex, 1975

Barrios, S. "Bancos y Tecnología." Caracas: Council for Scientific and Technological Development, 1976. Processed.

Chudson, W. A., and Louis T. Wells. "The Acquisition of Proprietary Technology by Developing Countries from Multinational Enterprises: A Review of Issues and Policies." New York: U.N. Department of Economic and Social Affairs, June 1973. Processed.

Cooper, C. M., and P. Maxwell. "Machinery Suppliers and the Transfer of Technology to Latin America." Report to the Department of Scientific Affairs, Organization of American States. Science Policy Research Unit, University of Sussex, 1975. Processed.

Cooper, C. M., and N. Clark. *The Transfer of Technology to Latin America.* Doc. No. ScA/PS-1. Washington, D.C.: Department of Scientific Affairs, Organization of American States, 1972.

Cooper, C. M., and F. Sercovitch. *The Channels and Mechanisms for the Transfer of Technology from Developed to Developing Countries.* TR/B/AC 11/5. Geneva: UNCTAD, April 1971.

Dahlman, Carl J., and Larry E. Westphal. "The Meaning of Technological Mastery in Relation to Transfer of Technology." *Annals of the American Academy of Political and Social Science,* vol. 458 (Fall 1981).

Ecosipro Ltd. "Investigación sobre la Política de Compras de Bienes de Capital en los Sectores Petroquímico y Siderúrgico." Caracas, June 1976. Processed.

Gabriel, P. "The International Transfer of Corporate Skills: Management Contracts in Developing Countries." Division of Research, Harvard University Graduate School of Business Administration, 1967.

Giral, José B., and R. P. Morgan. "Appropriate Technology for Chemical Industries in Developing Countries." Report prepared in connection with Foreign Area Fellowship Programme held at National Autonomous University of Mexico, Mexico City, July-August 1972.

Johnson, H. G. *Technology and Economic Interdependence.* London: Macmillan Press Ltd., for the Trade Policy Research Centre, 1975.

Judet, P., and J. Perrin. "A Propos du Transfert des Technologies pour un Programme Intégral de Développement Industriel." Grenoble: Institut de Recherche Economique et Planification–UNIDO, June 1971.

Junta del Acuerdo de Cartagena. "Desagregación del Paquete Tecnológico." J/GT-11/Rev. 1. Lima, March 1974.

———. "Policies Relating to the Transfer of Technology of the Countries of the Andean Pact: Their Foundations." Paper presented at the Third Session, UNCTAD, Santiago de Chile, 1972.

Kamenetzky, M., and F. Sercovitch. "Transferencia de Tecnología en la Industria Química Argentina." Paper presented at the Centro de Investigación de la Pequeña y Mediana Industria, Instituto Nacional de Tecnología Industrial, Buenos Aires, 1974. Processed.

McCulloch, Rachel. "Technology Transfer to Developing Countries: Implications of International Regulation." *Annals of the American Academy of Political and Social Science*, vol. 458 (Fall 1981).

Nadal, A. "Política Tecnológica de la Empresa Estatal Petróleos Mexicanos." Mexico City: Colegio de México, 1976. Processed.

National Science Foundation. "The Effects of International Transfer in the U.S. Economy." Papers and proceedings of a colloquium, Washington, D.C., November, 1973.

Organization of American States (OAS). "Estudio Comparativo de las Legislaciones Latinoamericanas sobre Regulación y Control de la Inversión Privada Extranjera." Ser 6, CP/INF; 680/75, Rev. 1. Washington, D.C., November 1975.

Organisation for Economic Co-operation and Development. (OECD). *North-South Technology Transfer: The Way Ahead.* Paris, 1981.

Punto Focal Nacional de Venezuela. "Selección y Evaluación de Esquemas Tecnológicos Alternativos y Negociación de Licencias para un Complejo Petroquímico." Paper presented at a working meeting of the chemical and petrochemical sector in Quito. Washington, D.C.: Department of Scientific Affairs, Organization of American States, April 1975.

———. "Estudios sobre Proyectos de Inversión." Paper presented at a working meeting of the chemical and petrochemical sector in Quito. Washington, D.C.: Department of Scientific Affairs, Organization of American States, April 1975.

Reni, Luciano. "La Transferencia de Tecnología en la Industria Petroquímica Básica Nacional." Caracas: Centro de Estudios de la Administración Pública, Universidad Central de Venezuela, July 1975. Processed.

Schaffel, G. "Transferring Licensed Process Technology." *Chemical Engineering*, April 20, 1970.

Stewart, Frances. *International Technology Transfer: Issues and Policy Options.* World Bank Staff Working Paper no. 344. Washington, D.C., 1979.

———. "Technology and Employment in LDCs." Paper prepared for the Ford Conference, Delhi, March 1973.

Stobaugh, Robert B. "The International Transfer of Technology in the Establishment of the Petrochemical Industry in Developing Countries." United Nations Institute for Training and Research, Research Report no. 12. New York, 1971.

———. "Utilizing Technical Know-how in a Foreign Investment and Licensing Programme." Proceedings of the Chemical Marketing Research Association, Houston, Texas, February 1970.

Tavares de Araujo, J., and Vera Maria Dick. "The Government, Multinational Enterprises and National Enterprises: The Case of the Brazilian Petrochemical Industry." *Pesquisa e Planejamento Econômico*, vol. 4, no. 3 (December 1974).

Teece, David J. "The Market for Know-How and the Efficient International Transfer of Technology." *Annals of the American Academy of Political and Social Science*, vol. 458 (Fall 1981).

United Nations Conference on Trade and Development (UNCTAD). "Major Issues in Transfer of Technology to Developing Countries." TD/AC 11/10. Geneva, 1974.

———. "Principales Cuestiones que Plantea la Transmisión de Technología: Estudio Monográfico sobre Chile." TD/B/AC. 11/20. Geneva, May 1974.

———. "Restrictive Business Practices." TD/B/C.2/93. Geneva, 1970.

United Nations. "The Acquisition of Technology from Multinational Corporations by Developing Countries." E.74.II.A.7. New York, 1974.

Vaitsos, C. "Transfer of Industrial Technology to Developing Countries through Private Enterprises." Study for the Board of the Cartagena Agreement, Lima and Bogotá, February 1970. Processed.

Vaitsos, C., and others. "Technology Policy and Economic Development." Summary report on studies undertaken by the Board of the Cartagena Agreement for the Andean Pact Integration Process. IDRC-061e. Ottawa: International Development Research Center, 1976.

Villanueva, M. A. "Comportamiento Tecnológico de las Empresas Mixtas en la Industria Petroquímica." Caracas: National Council for Scientific and Technical Research, June 1976. Processed.

Wada, M. "Economic Development in Japan and Transfer of Technology." Paper presented at the Catholic University, Santiago de Chile, May 1972.

———. "Japan's Petrochemical Technology: Efforts Used for Development of New Techniques Based on Imported Know-how." *Asahi Evening News*, special edition. Tokyo, 1971.

Wada, M. "Mechanisms for the Transfer of Modern Technology." Science Policy Research Unit, University of Sussex, April 1975. Processed.

Wionczek, M. S., and others. *La Transferencia Internacional de Tecnología: El Caso de México*. Mexico City: Fondo de Cultura Económica, 1974.

Technical Change

Achilladelis, B. "Process Innovation in the Chemical Industry." D.Phil. dissertation, University of Sussex, 1973.

Arrow, K. J. "The Economic Implications of Learning by Doing." *Review of Economic Studies*, July 1962.

———. "Economic Welfare and the Allocation of Resources for Invention." In R. R. Nelson, ed., *The Rate and Direction of Inventive Activity: Economic and Social Factors*. National Bureau of Economic Research, Special Conference Series no. 13. Princeton, N.J.: Princeton University Press, 1962.

Cooper, Charles M. *Policy Interventions for Technological Innovation in Developing Countries*. World Bank Staff Working Paper no. 441. Washington, D.C., 1980.

———. "The Effects of Innovation on Barriers to Entry and Internal Structure in a Sylos-Labini Oligopoly." Appendix I in C. Cooper, C. Freeman, and F. Sercovitch, "The British Patent System in Relation to the International Patent System and Developing Countries." Science Policy Research Unit, University of Sussex, September 1973. Processed.

———. "Science, Technology and Production in the Underdeveloped Countries: An Introduction." *Journal of Development Studies*, no. 9 (October, 1972).

———, ed. *Science, Technology and Development: The Political Economy of Technical Advance in Underdeveloped Countries*. London: Frank Cass, 1973.

de Santiago, Miguel. "La Tecnología en las Industrias Química y Petroquímica." Paper presented at the working meeting of the chemical and petrochemical sector in Quito. SG/P, PPTT/32-b.2. Washington, D.C.: Department of Scientific Affairs, Organization of American States, April 1975.

Enos, J. L. "Invention and Innovation in the Petroleum Refining Industry." In National Bureau of Economic Research, *The Rate and Direction of Inventive Activity*. Princeton, N.J.: Princeton University Press, 1962.

Freeman, C. "Chemical Process Plant: Innovation and the World Market." *National Institute Economic Review*, no. 45 (August 1968).

———. "The Plastics Industry: A Comparative Study of Research and Innovation." *National Institute Economic Review*, no. 26 (November 1963).

Gruber, W., D. Mehta, and R. Vernon. "The R and D Factor in International Trade and International Investment of United States Industries." *Journal of Political Economy*, vol. 75, no. 1 (1967), pp. 20–37.

Kahan, S. "Patents and Licensing in the Petrochemical Industry." In UNIDO, *Studies in Petrochemicals*.

Posner, M. V. "International Trade and Technical Change." *Oxford Economic Papers*, no. 13 (October, 1961).

Sábato, J. "Empresas y Fábricas de Tecnología." AC/PE-26. Washington, D.C.: Department of Scientific Affairs, Organization of American States, March 1972.

Sylos-Labini, P. *Oligopoly and Technical Progress*. Rev. ed. Cambridge, Mass.: Harvard University Press, 1959.

Tampier, J. "El Desarrollo Tecnológico del Japon." Report to the Junta del Acuerdo de Cartagena. J/AJ/38. Lima, March 1973.

Vianna, Dulce M. (Grupo Rio de Janeiro). "Technological Research at Petrobras." Report prepared for the Science and Technology Policy Instruments Study sponsored by the International Development Research Center of Canada. Rio de Janeiro, 1975. Processed.

Walker, W. "Industrial Innovation and International Trading Performance." Science Policy Research Unit, University of Sussex, October 1975. Processed.

Chemical and Petrochemical Industry

Acosta Hermoso, E. "Development of the Petrochemical Industry in Venezuela." In UNIDO, *Petrochemical Industries in Developing Countries*.

American Chemical Society. *Chemistry in the Economy*. Washington, D.C., 1973.

Baker, G. R. "The Development of a Joint Petrochemical Venture in Chile: The Petrodow Project, A Case History. In UNIDO, *Problems and Prospects of the Chemical Industries in the Less Developed Countries*.

Becerra Neto, J. "The Fertiliser Industry of Brasil." In UNIDO, *Second Interregional Fertiliser Symposium*.

Berenguer, F., and others. "Situación Actual y Planes para el Futuro de la Industria de los Plásticos en Colombia." In UNIDO, *Simposio sobre el Desarrollo de las Industrias de Transformación*.

Behrens, A. "Alguno Aspectos de la Industria Petroquímica en los Paises de la Asociación Latino-Americana de Libre Comercio." In UNIDO, *Simposio sobre el Desarrollo de las Industrias de Transformación*.

Benton, Alan. *Selection of Projects and Production Processes for Basic and Intermediate Petrochemicals in Developing Countries*. Petrochemical Industry Series. Monograph no. 2. New York: United Nations, 1969.

Brandao, E., and others. "The Petrochemical Industry in Brazil." In UNIDO, *Studies in Petrochemicals*.

Bosque, E., and R. P. Peregrina. "The Fertiliser Industry of Mexico." In UNIDO, *Second Interregional Fertiliser Symposium.*

De Podwin, H. J., and Associates, Inc. "Comparative Costs of Entry into the United States and European Markets." February 1966. Quoted by A. D. Amery, "The Economic Implications of the World of Petrochemicals." In *The Shrinking World of Petrochemicals.* Washington, D.C.: American Chemical Society, May 1970.

de Santiago, Miguel, and Oscar R. Bourguin. "La Industria Petroquímica." *Revista de la Universidad* (Buenos Aires) 1974.

De Souza, H. "The Petrochemical Industry: Peru." In UNIDO, *Studies in Petro-chemicals.*

Duff, B. S. "New Primary Feed Stock Supplier Accelerates Development of Large Scale Petrochemical Industry in Brazil." In UNIDO, *Petrochemical Industries in Developing Countries.*

Economic Commission for Latin America (ECLA). "Las Industrias Químicas en America Latina y su Evolución entre 1959 y 1967." E/CN.12 1848. New York: United Nations, February 1970.

———. *The Manufacture of Industrial Machinery and Equipment in Latin America.* Vol. 1. *Basic Equipment in Brazil.* New York: United Nations, 1963.

Garay Salamanca, C. "Situación Actual y Planes para el Futuro de la Industria de los Plásticos en el Grupo Andino." In UNIDO, *Simposio sobre el Desarrollo de las Industrias de Transformación.*

Gersumky, W., and A. E. Abrahams. "Joint Venture and Acquisition Analysis in Brazil. In UNIDO, *Problems and Prospects of the Chemical Industries in Less Developed Countries.*

Goho, T. S. "The Petrochemical Industry." In Jeve Behrman, *The Role of International Companies in Latin American Integration: Autos and Petrochem-icals.* Lexington, Mass.: D. C. Heath, 1972.

Gomez Prada, A. "Instalación de una Planta de Caprolactama en Colombia." Paper presented at a working meeting of the chemical and petrochemical sector in Quito. Washington, D.C.: Department of Scientific Affairs, Organization of American States, April 1975.

Hahn, Albert. *The Brazilian Synthetic Polymer Industry.* Petrochemical Industry Series. Monograph no. 1. New York: United Nations, 1969.

Heath, F. J. "The Changing Economics of the Fertilizer Industry." In *World Petrochemicals.* Conference organized by the *Financial Times* in association with the *Oil Daily,* London and New York, February 5–6, 1975.

Huambachano, M. "The Fertiliser Industry of Peru." In UNIDO, *Second Inter-regional Fertiliser Symposium.*

Hughlett, Lloyd J. *Industrialisation of Latin America.* New York: McGraw-Hill, 1946.

Innes, T. J. "The Effects of the Increased Oil Costs." In *World Petrochemicals.*

Conference organized by the *Financial Times* in association with the *Oil Daily*, London and New York, February 5–6, 1975.

Instituto Venezolano de Petroquímica (IVP). "Aporte del Instituto Venezolano de Petroquímica al Desarrollo Agropecuario Nacional." Caracas, August 1969. Processed.

———. "Condiciones de Financiamiento de las Empresas Mixtas." Caracas: Subdirección General de Empresas Mixtas, IVP, July 1974. Processed.

———. "Información sobre Empresas Mixtas, Nuevos Proyectos y Requerimientos de Productos Básicos." Caracas: Dirección Técnica Gerencia Control de Proyectos, IVP, February 1975. Processed.

Infante, Miguel A. "Los Fertilizantes en Colombia." Bogotá: Fondo Colombiano de Investigaciones Científicas, June 1975. Processed.

Kovacevich, M. A. "The Present Status and Future Plans for Development of the Plastics Industry in Argentina." Symposium on Plastics Industries in a Developing World, June 18–20, 1973. London: Plastics Institute, 1973. Processed.

Lipphardtt, G. "Current Problems in the European Petrochemical Industry." In *World Petrochemicals*. Conference organized by the *Financial Times* in association with the *Oil Daily*, London and New York, February 5–6, 1975.

McCurdy, P. "Foreign Trade, Investments, Plants Push Chemical Industry Towards Integrated World Wide Operation." *Chemical and Engineering News*, April 16, 1973, pp. 20–28.

McLean, John. "Financing Overseas Expansion." *Harvard Business Review* (March-April 1963).

Mosso, N., E. Amadeo, and R. Fernández. "La Industria Petroquímica Argentina." Buenos Aires: Consejo Latino-Americano de Ciencias Sociales, 1976. Processed.

Nardini, C. H. "Situación Actual y Planes Para el Futuro de la Industria de los Plásticos en Argentina." In UNIDO, *Simposio sobre el Desarrollo de las Industrias de Transformación*.

Otero Rusanova, G. "The Venezuelan Petrochemical Industry." In UNIDO, *Studies in Petrochemicals*.

Perroni, O. V. "Development of the Petrochemical Industry in Brazil." In UNIDO, *Petrochemical Industries in Developing Countries*.

Petróleos Mexicanos. "Structure of Petrochemical Development in Mexico: Reynosa and Pajaritos Developments." In UNIDO, *Studies in Petrochemicals*.

———. "The Mexican Government and the Petrochemical Industry in Mexico." In UNIDO, *Studies in Petrochemicals*.

Petroquisa. *Polo Petroquímico do Nordeste*. Brasília, October 1974.

Ramos, Oliveira. "Present Status and Future Plans of the Plastics Industry in Brazil." In UNIDO, *Simposio sobre el Desarrollo de las Industrias de Transformación*.

Rueben, B. G., and M. L. Burstall. *The Chemical Economy*. London: Long-mans, 1973.

Salinas, W. "Situación Actual y Planes para el Futuro de la Industria de los Plásticos en el Perú." In UNIDO, *Simposio sobre el Desarrollo de las Industrias de Tranformación*.

Schiffino, R. "Problems and Prospects of the Petrochemical Industry in Brazil." In UNIDO, *Problems and Prospects of the Chemical Industries in Less Developed Countries*.

Shell Chemical Co. *Economics of Chemicals from Petroleum*. London, 1971.

Simian, E. G. "Development of the Petrochemical Industry in Chile." In UNIDO, *Petrochemical Industries in Developing Countries*.

Sittenfield, M. "Prospects for Chemical Industrial Development within the Andean Subregional Common Market." In UNIDO, *Problems and Prospects of the Chemical Industries in Less Developed Countries*.

United Nations Industrial Development Organization (UNIDO). "Experts Group Meeting on the Development of the Synthetic Rubber Industry," Snagov, Romania, June 25–29, 1973. ID/Wg.158.

―――. *Petrochemical Industries in Developing Countries*. Interregional Petrochemical Symposium, Baku, U.S.S.R., October 21–31, 1969. 7011.B.23. New York: United Nations, 1970.

―――. *The Petrochemical Industry*. ID/106. New York, 1973.

―――. *Problems and Prospects of the Chemical Industries in the Less Developed Countries: Case Histories*. Symposium sponsored by the Division of Chemical Marketing and Economics in cooperation with UNIDO at the 158th meeting of the American Chemical Society, New York, September 8–11, 1969.

―――. *Studies in Petrochemicals*. Conference held at Tehran, Iran, November 16–30, 1964. ST/CID/4. New York: United Nations.

―――. *Second Inter-regional Fertiliser Symposium*. Kiev, U.S.S.R., September 21–October 1, 1971; New Delhi, India, October 2–13, 1971. ID/WG.99. New York: United Nations.

―――. *Simposio sobre el Desarrollo de las Industrias de Transformación de Materiales Plásticos en America Latina*. Bogotá, November 20–December 1, 1972. ID/WG.137. New York: United Nations.

Villanueva, M. "Comportamiento Tecnológico de las Empresas Mixtas en la Industria Petroquímica." Caracas: Consejo Nacional de Investigaciones Cien-tíficas y Tecnológicas, June 1976. Processed.

Wada, M. "The Role of General Trading Companies as a New Type of Multina-tional Enterprise in the Foreign Investment of the Japanese Petrochemical Industry." Science Policy Research Unit, University of Sussex, February 1975. Processed.

Waddams, A. L. *Chemicals from Petroleum: An Industry Survey*. New York: Wiley, 1973.

Wesser, F. "Manufacturing of Chemical Plant Equipment." Paper presented at the UNIDO-DECHEMA Seminar on Operation, Maintenance and Manufacturing of Chemical Plants and Equipment in Developing Countries. ID/WG.60/6. New York: UNIDO, June 1970. Processed.

Yanno. "Proyecto de Estudio de la Industria Petroquímica Básica en Latinamérica." Bariloche: Comisión Económica para América Latina, 1972. Processed.

Engineering and Consultancy

Alves, Sergio F., and Ecila M. Ford. "O Comportamento das Empresas Estatais: A Seleção das Empresas de Engineering, a Escolha de Processos Industriais e a Compra de Bens de Capital." Study prepared by the Grupo de Pesquisas, Financiadora Nacional de Estudos e Projetos, São Paulo, June 1975. Processed.

Brown, M. *Engineering of Industrial Projects*. OECD Development Centre, Occasional Paper no. 11. CD-T1, (76)4. Paris, 1976.

Brooks, K. "The U.S. Engineering Construction Industry: Is It Ready for a Building Boom?" *Chemical Week*, March 21, 1973.

Castillo A. del. "Demandas de Equipo para las Plantas de Petróleos Mexicanos." Memoria del Primer Congreso de la Asociación Nacional de Firmas de Ingeniería, Mexico City, 1971.

de La Vega Navarro, A. "La Société Nationale Mexicaine Pemex et l'Engineering." Grenoble: Institut de Recherche Economique et Planification, Université des Sciences Sociales de Grenoble, December 1970.

de La Vega Navarro, A., and J. Perrin. "Desarrollo y Fortalecimiento de la Ingeniería en México." Mexico City: Colegio de México, December 1974. Processed.

Institut de Recherche Economique et Planification (IREP). "Le Développement des Capacités d'Engineering en Algérie." Rapport de Synthèse, Ministère de l'Industrie et de l'Energie. Algérie, February 1973.

Judet, P., J. Perrin, and R. Tibergein. "L'Engineering: Rapport Provisoire." IREP, Université des Sciences Sociales de Grenoble, May 1970.

Kamenetzky, M. "Process Engineering and Process Industries in Argentina and Mexico." Study sponsored by the International Development Research Center of Canada. Buenos Aires, 1976. Processed.

———. "Engineering and Pre-investment work." Study sponsored by the International Development Research Center of Canada. Buenos Aires, 1976. Processed.

Malhotra, A. K. "Consulting and Engineering Design Capability in Developing Countries." Report prepared for the Science and Technology Policy Instruments Study sponsored by the International Development Research Center of Canada. Ottawa, July 1976. Processed.

Nadal, A. "Engineering Firms in Mexico." Mexico City: Colegio de México, May 1976. Processed.

Perrin, J. "Engineering, Technologie et Fonction Economique." Paris: OECD, February 1976. Processed.

―――. "Place et Fonction de l'Engineering dans le Système Industriel Français." IREP, Université des Sciences Sociales de Grenoble, March 1973.

Peruvian Group. "La Situación de la Actividad de Ingeniería en el Perú." Report prepared for the Science and Technology Policy Instruments Study sponsored by the International Development Research Center of Canada. Lima: Oficina Nacional de Planificación, October 1975. Processed.

Politzer, K. "Projeto de Processamento." Paper presented at the Simposium Semana de Tecnologia Industrial, sponsored by Ministerio de Indústria e Comércio, São Paulo, September 1975.

Roberts, J. "Engineering Consultancy, Industrialization and Development." In C. Cooper, ed., *Science, Technology and Development*. London: Frank Cass, 1973.

Suarez, F. L., and Stuhlman. "Análisis de las Firmas de Ingeniería para Industrias de Procesos en Argentina." Buenos Aires: CLACSO, December 1975. Processed.

Yanez, Gonzalez J. "La Ingeniería de Procesos en la Empresa Nacional del Petróleo." *Revista de la Empresa Nacional del Petróleo*. Santiago, 1975.

Yen, Ye-Chen. "Estimating Plant Costs in the Developing Countries." *Chemical Engineering*, July 10, 1972.

Corporate Strategy and Foreign Investment

Barnet, R., and R. Muller. *Global Reach: The Power of the Multinational Corporations*. New York: Simon and Schuster, 1974.

Franko, L. G. *Joint Venture Survival in Multinational Corporations*. New York, London: Praeger, 1971.

Helleiner, G. K. "Transnational Enterprises in the Manufacturing Sector of Less Developed Countries." University of Toronto, 1975. Processed.

Hirsch, S. *Location of Industry and International Competitiveness*. Oxford: Clarendon Press, 1967.

―――. "The United States Electronics Industry in International Trade." *National Institute Economic Review*, no. 34 (November 1965).

Hufbauer, C. G. *Synthetic Materials and the Theory of International Trade*. Cambridge, Mass.: Harvard University Press, 1966.

Marris, R. *Theory of Managerial Capitalism*. London: Macmillan, 1964.

Schelling, T. *The Strategy of Conflict*. Cambridge, Mass.: Harvard University Press, 1960.

Stobaugh, R. B. "The Product Life Cycle, U.S. Exports and International Investment." D.B.A. dissertation, Harvard University Graduate School of Business Administration, 1968.

Streeten, P. "The Dynamics of the New Poor Power." In G. Helleiner, ed., *A World Divided: The Less Developed Countries in the International Economy*. New York: Cambridge University Press, 1976.

Vaitsos, C. "Power, Knowledge and Development Policy: Relations between Transnational Enterprises and Developing Countries." In G. Helleiner, ed., *A World Divided: The Less Developed Countries in the International Economy*. New York: Cambridge University Press, 1976.

————. *Intercountry Income Distribution and Transnational Enterprises*. Oxford: Clarendon Press, 1974.

Vaupel, J., and Joan P. Curham. "The Making of a Multinational Enterprise." Boston, Mass.: Division of Research, Graduate School of Business Administration, Harvard University, 1973.

Vernon, Raymond. "International Investment and International Trade in the Product Cycle." *Quarterly Journal of Economics*, vol. 80, no. 1 (May 1966).

Wells, Louis T., Jr., ed. *The Product Life Cycle and International Trade*. Boston, Mass.: Graduate School of Business Administration, Harvard University, 1972.

Trade and Trade Policies

Balassa, B., and Associates. *The Structure of Protection in Developing Countries*. Baltimore, Md.: Johns Hopkins University Press, 1971.

Business International. "Recent Experience in Establishing Joint Ventures: Latin America." Management Monographs no. 54. New York, 1972. Pp. 11–26.

Corden, W. M. "The Structure of a Tariff System and the Effective Protective Rate." *Journal of Political Economy*, vol. 74 (June 1966), pp. 221–37.

Statistical Methods

Blalock, Hubert M. *Social Statistics*. 2d ed., New York: McGraw-Hill, 1972.

Roulon, P. J., and W. D. Brooks. "On Statistical Tests of Group Differences." In D. K. Whitla, *Measurement and Assessment in the Behavioral Sciences*. Reading, Mass.: Addison-Wesley, 1968.

Trade Journal Sources of Information on Plant Ownership and Technology Suppliers

Business Latin America. All 1972 and 1973 issues.

Chemical Age International. "Surveys of Export Contracts," June 19, 1970; June 25, 1971; June 16, 1972; and June 15, 1973.

Chemical Week. (McGraw-Hill Publications.) "Annual Plant Register."

Hydrocarbon Processing. (Gulf Publishing Company, formerly Hydrocarbon Processing and Petroleum Refiner.) "Construction Box Score" (quarterly).

Oil and Gas Journal. (Petroleum Publishing Company.) "World-wide Survey of Petrochemical Facilities" (annual).

Quarterly Economic Review. (Economic Intelligence Unit, London.) Nos. 1–4, 1973.

World-wide Petrochemical Directory. (Petroleum Publishing Company, Tulsa.) Annual.

Note: We also screened the issues published since 1970 of other trade journals such as *Petróleo y Petroquímica Internacional*, *European Chemical News*, and *Chemical and Engineering News*.

Index

The full range of World Bank publications, both free and for sale, is described in the *Catalog of Publications*; the continuing research program is outlined in *Abstracts of Current Studies*. Both booklets are updated annually; the most recent edition of each is available without charge from the Publications Sales Unit, Department B, The World Bank, 1818 H Street, N.W., Washington, D.C. 20433, U.S.A.

Mariluz Cortes is an industrial economist in the East Africa Projects Department of the World Bank, and Peter Bocock is a consultant in the Development Research Department of the Bank.